MEDITERRANEAN DIET COOKBOOK FOR BEGINNERS 2023

1500 Effortless Delicious Recipes to Change your Eating Lifestyle for Lifelong Health

By
Alexandra Bryne

DISCLAIMER

The information written in this book is for educational and entertainment purposes only. Strenuous efforts have been made to provide accurate, up to date and reliable complete information. The information in this book is true and complete to the best of our knowledge. All recommendations are made without guarantee on the part of the author and publisher.

Neither the publisher nor the author takes any responsibility for any possible consequences of reading or enjoying the recipes in this book. The author and publisher disclaim any liability in connection with the use of information contained in this book. Under no circumstance will any legal responsibility or blame be apportioned against the author or publisher for any reparation, damages, or monetary loss due to the information herein, either directly or indirectly.

Table of Contents

INTRODUCTION

Meaning of Mediterranean Diet

A Mediterranean diet is a diet of many Mediterranean countries such as Italy and Greece that are mainly of cereals, grains, vegetables, beans, fruits, and nuts with reasonable quantity of fish, cheese, olive oil, and wine. It is usually followed in Greece, Crete, Spain, and parts of Italy that emphasizes fruits and vegetables, nuts, grains, olive oil instead of butter and grilled chicken and seafood with a glass of red wine. Mediterranean diet makes use of fruits, bread, vegetables, cereals, beans, nuts and seeds. Olive oil is used instead of butter and Dairy products, fish and poultry are eaten in moderate quantity. In terms of meat, small quantity is eaten while eggs are at least zero to four times a week.

Scientists stated that a Mediterranean diet plays a good role in the prevention of coronary artery heart disease. It also appears to aid stay away from the metabolic syndrome.

History of the Mediterranean Diet

The countries that have originated the Mediterranean diet comprise all countries that surround the Mediterranean Sea. In Europe, parts of Italy, Greece, Portugal and Spain stick to ethics of the Mediterranean Diet. Parts of the Balkan region and Turkey follow the diet, as well as Middle Eastern countries like Lebanon and Syria. The warm temperature of the Mediterranean region makes them produce large fresh fruits and vegetables almost year round that people eat across the globe. Bread, olive oil, wine, nuts, and legumes are other food of the region.

However, the diet of the Mediterranean basin about 22countries along the bounds of Africa, Europe, and Asia is rich in foods of plant origin such as legumes, fruits and vegetables, and olive oil as a major basis of fat and consumes minimal saturated fat. There are some few local differences and similarities in terms of patterns of diet around the Mediterranean Sea. Over many decades, Mediterranean diet's origins reflect the relations of various populations and civilizations.

Diet is one of the most important risk factors within our control. This is found about 30% and 20% of the population risk for heart disease and stroke respectively. In modern history, a lot of research has been done concerning the dietary pattern of Mediterranean. Cognitive interest on the Mediterranean diet and lifestyle began in the late 1950s when scientists spotted that Italy, Spain, Southern France, Greece and Turkey experienced fewer deaths from heart disease as found in other countries. They finally resolved that low in takes of saturated fat were the major diet's features that sheltered the hearts of people in the region.

The Mediterranean diet has low saturated fat and is regarded as a low-fat diet. Moderate intake of wine and alcohol and lively lifestyles also define the traditional Mediterranean way of life.

The Science Behind the Mediterranean Diet

The Mediterranean diet is a current food representation adopted by the usual food patterns of some of the countries of the Mediterranean region, mostly Greece, Cyprus, Portugal, Southern Italy, Turkey and Spain.
Shared features to the diets of these countries are a high consumption of fruit and vegetables, bread and other cereals, olive oil and fish, making those people low in saturated fat and high in dietary fibre.
A major feature in the demand of the Mediterranean Diet is its richness and sweet flavoured foods. Margarine and other butter are considered tasteless and missing the flavour that olive oil gives to meals. Red wine is also taken often but in reasonable quantities. It has been scientifically proven that Mediterranean Diet is one of the low carb diets.

Health Benefits of Eating the Mediterranean Diet

The following are health benefits of eating the Mediterranean diet; consistently eating the Mediterranean diet exposes us to some benefits that are associated with our health and happy living:

1. **Mediterranean Diet Aids in Preserving Loss of Memory.**

The Mediterranean diet is very good for developing brain power and preventing loss of memory because it is rich in healthy fats for the brain. Researchers and their studies suggest that high devotion to a Mediterranean diet is associated with a 40% reduced risk for loss of memory.

2. **Mediterranean Diet Has Capacity to Manage Diabetes and Blood Sugar Level.**

Researchers have proven that Mediterranean diet has helpful effects for diabetes. In particular, type 2 diabetes can be manage and also help improve blood sugar control. It may not give total cure to diabetes but it can help in managing the sickness.

3. **Mediterranean Diet Aids in Fighting Depression.**

Individuals who adhere to the Mediterranean diet can be protected against depression. Research confirms that a person who follows Mediterranean diet most strictly has lower threat of developing depression.

4. **Mediterranean Diet Guard Against Cancer.**

High consistency to a Mediterranean Diet can help protect against cancer. Research discovers that people who stick to the diet mainly have a 13% rate of cancer death. Particular cancers guarded against include breast cancer, prostate cancer, liver cancer, colorectal cancer, neck cancer and gastric cancer.

5. **Mediterranean Diet Aids in Reducing Your Risk of Having Heart Disease.**

According to research, a Mediterranean diet can significantly cut your risk of having cardiovascular disease, such as myocardial infarction, stroke and coronary heart disease.

This is probably as a result of the Mediterranean diet's helpful effects on cardiovascular risk features, such as high blood pressure, triglycerides, and cholesterol. To reduce risk of having Heart disease, Mediterranean diet is a strong recommendation.

6. **Mediterranean Diet Aids in Strengthening Bones.**

According to scientific research, some important elements in olive oil can help in preserving bone density by increasing the large number and give strong bone. Nutritional guide associated with the Mediterranean diet may help to guard against osteoporosis.

7. **Eating Mediterranean Diet May Reduce Women's Risk for Partial Stroke.**

Eating Mediterranean Diet can help to decrease the risk of cardiovascular disease in some women. Well, the diet can also help reduce stroke risk in women. The more closely a woman follows a Mediterranean Diet, the lower the risk of having a stroke.

8. **The Mediterranean Diet May Help In Weight Loss and Maintenance.**

Likely due to its focus on whole grain and fresh foods, the Mediterranean Diet may help you drastically lose weight in a sustainable way.

Delicious Path to Weight Loss on Mediterranean diet

Here are some tips that will guide you to weight loss on Mediterranean diet.

1. **Eating foods that are main meals should be taken in the early hours of the day.**

Usually in a Mediterranean diet, lunch is the major food. By eating a larger meal early in the day, you reduce the risk of overeating later. According to research people who ate their largest meal before 3 pm are the ones who will lose more weight compared to those that eat largest meal beyond 3pm.

2. **Eat vegetables regularly and as your main food cooked in olive oil.**

When eating a vegetable dish cooked in olive oil and tomato you are taking 4 portions of vegetables in one sitting. Mediterranean dishes are not high in calories but are low in carbs. An added benefit of eating vegetables is that you will avoid drowsiness because it is not a carb rich meal.

3. **Drink mostly water and sometimes tea, coffee and wine for adults.**

In Mediterranean diet you should drink water, rather than milk and yoghurt. To lose weight with Mediterranean diet water must be taken mostly. At times adults could drink tea, coffee and wine while eating, as it aids in weight lose too.

4. **Eat moderate quantity of olive oil.**

Olive oil not only makes all those vegetables delicious, it makes the meal filling. It gives a nice flavour and makes our meal nutritious. It also aids in weight loss.

Foods to Eat on Mediterranean Diet

Your diet should be according to these healthy and natural Mediterranean foods:

1. **Eggs**:

Chicken, duck eggs and quail.

2. **Dairy**:

Cheese and Greek yogurt

3. **Spices and Herbs**:

Mint, Garlic, basil, rosemary, sage, nutmeg, cinnamon, pepper

4. **Healthy Fats**:

Olives, Extra virgin olive oil, avocados and avocado oil

5. **Drinks:**

Water, Red wine, Coffee, Tea

6. **Vegetables**:

Spinach, onions, cauliflower, Tomatoes, broccoli, kale, carrots, Brussels sprouts, cucumbers

7. **Fruits**:

Apples, bananas, oranges, pears, strawberries, grapes, dates, figs, melons, peaches

8. **Nuts and Seed**s:

Macadamia nuts, hazelnuts, cashews, Almonds, walnuts, sunflower seeds, pumpkin seeds

9. **Legumes**:

Lentils, pulses, Beans, peas, peanuts, and chickpeas

10. **Tubers**:

Potatoes, turnip, yam

11. **Whole grains**:

Barley, corn, buckwheat, Whole oats, brown rice, rye, whole wheat, whole-grain bread and pasta

12. **Fish and Seafood**:

Tuna, mackerel, Salmon, sardines, trout, shrimp, oysters, clams, crab, mussels

13. **Poultry**:

Turkey, chicken, and duck

Foods to Avoid on Mediterranean Diet

You should avoid these foods while on Mediterranean diet:

1. **Tran's Fats:**

Found in margarine and processed foods.

2. **Refined Oils:**

Canola oil, Soybean oil, cottonseed oil etc

3. **Processed Meat:**

Processed sausages, and hot dogs

4. **Highly Processed Foods:**

Food labelled low- fat and which is factory-made.

5. **Added Sugar:**

Ice cream, Soda, candies, table sugar, and others

6. **Refined Grains:**

Pasta made with refined wheat and White bread etc.

Tips for Success on Mediterranean Diet

1. **Change Your Oil:**

Switch vegetable oil and coconut oil to extra-virgin olive oil because olive oil is loaded in monounsaturated fatty acids; according to a 2017 study it may improve HDL cholesterol being the best type of cholesterol. You can sprinkle it on finished foods like fish and chicken. Change butter for olive oil in mashed potatoes, pasta.

2. **Eat Lots of Fish:**

Fish is rich in protein in the Mediterranean diet. Especially, fishes like salmon, sardines and mackerel. These fish are rich in heart and brain healthy fatty acids. Smaller fishes that are thinner and have less fat are also good because they are good source of protein.

3. **Eat Veggies Almost Everyday:**

If your diet lacks vegetables, put in more veggies. To do this, eat one serving at snack time, like putting a handful of spinach into a smoothie and one at dinner. Target at least two servings per day. According to Australian research, at least three servings can help you bust stress.

4. **Snack on Nuts:**

This is another Mediterranean diet staple. Nuts include almonds, cashews and pistachios. This can give you some satisfactions. Studies show that if people replaced their snack with almonds, their level of calories, added sugar and sodium will be lower. Nuts have more fibre and minerals for example potassium compared to processed snack foods.

5. **Savour Every Bite:**

Do not rush to eat your meal, calmly sit down at the table with your family and friends and eat properly. It gives you comfort. You will enjoy your company and your food. Eating slowly also gives a lot of satisfaction to your body.

6. **Choose Fruit for Dessert:**

Fruit is a good source of fibre, vitamin C and antioxidants. It helps you to eat more, add a little sugary slice of pear with honey. Always have fruit at your reach in order to satisfy your taste.

7. **Sip a Little Wine:**

The Mediterranean people are known for their consistent drinking of wine to quench their taste. It doesn't mean you should get drunk. It is strongly advised by the Dieticians who developed the Mediterranean diet that women should stick to a 3 Oz. serving, and men to a 5 Oz. serving per day.

8. **Eat Whole Grains:**

Go with grains that are in their whole form and unrefined. Quinoa does not take enough time to cook. It can be cooked in just 20 minutes, making it a great side dish. Use hot oat meal which is best for breakfast on a cold winter morning. Popcorn is also a whole grain. Complement your intake with other whole grain products, like whole wheat bread and pasta.

Mediterranean Diet Shopping Guide

Below is a simple shopping list to help you begin the Mediterranean Diet.

1. **Vegetables**: Broccoli, spinach, Carrots, onions, kale, garlic
2. **Fruits**: Oranges, grapes, Apples, and bananas
3. **Dairy**: Cheese, Greek yogurt.
4. **Eggs**: Chicken, Pastured enriched eggs.
5. **Oil**: Olive oil.
6. **Berries**: Blueberries and Strawberries
7. **Frozen veggies**: Select combination of healthy vegetables.
8. **Grains**: Whole-grain pasta and Whole-grain bread,
9. **Legumes**: Lentils, pulses, beans.
10. **Nuts**: Cashews, Almonds, walnuts.
11. **Fish**: Shellfish, salmon, sardines, mackerel, trout, shrimp.
12. **Tubers**: Sweet potatoes, yam, and Potatoes
13. **Seeds**: Sunflower seeds, pumpkin seeds.
14. **Condiments**: Cinnamon, sea salt, pepper, turmeric.

Eating Out on the Mediterranean Diet

The actual food that belongs to the Mediterranean Diet is a great disagreement on global scene. Different countries have their different diet but the focus is on healthy plant foods. Eat the following foods while eating out on Mediterranean Diet with your family and friends:

1. **Oil and Fat**: Extra virgin olive oil, Avocado oil.
2. **Fruits**: Blueberries, grapes, apricots, apples, Bananas, oranges, Peaches, strawberries, raspberries etc.
3. **Whole grains**: pasta, Whole-grain bread, Couscous, barley, corn, Oatmeal etc.
4. **Eggs**: Chicken, and duck eggs.
5. **Dairy**: Plain ricotta, Plain Greek yogurt, feta, goat cheese.
6. **Legumes**: Beans, lentils etc.
7. **Vegetables**: Artichokes, garlic, broccoli, carrots, onions, spinach, Eggplant, bell peppers, zucchini, and etc.
8. **Fish and seafood**: Mackerel, Shrimp, salmon, oysters, Sardines, etc.
9. **Poultry**: Duck, Chicken, turkey etc.
10. **Herbs and spices**: Cinnamon, pepper, garlic, basil, all herbs that are dried and fresh, Spices
11. **Tubers**: Turnips, yams, sweet potatoes, etc.
12. **Nuts and seeds**: Pistachios, cashews, walnuts, almonds etc.

Chapter 1: Breakfast Recipes

Breakfast Yogurt Sundae

Prep Time: 5 minutes
Servings: 1-2

Recipe Ingredients:

- ¾ cup of plain Greek yogurt
- ¼ cup of fresh mixed berries (blueberries, strawberries, blackberries)
- 2 tablespoons of walnut pieces
- 1 tablespoon of ground flaxseed
- 2 fresh mint leaves, shredded

Cooking Instruction:

1. Pour the yogurt into a tall parfait glass and sprinkle with the mixed berries, walnut pieces, and flaxseed.

2. Then, garnish with the shredded mint leaves and serve immediately.

Avocado Toast with Goat Cheese

Prep Time: 5 minutes
Cooking Time: 2 to 3 minutes
Servings: 2

Recipe Ingredients:

- 2 slices whole-wheat thin-sliced bread
- ½ avocado
- 2 tablespoons of crumbled goat cheese
- Salt, to taste

Cooking Instruction:

1. To begin, toast the bread slices in a toaster for 2 to 3 minutes on each side until browned.

2. Then, scoop out the flesh from the avocado into a medium bowl and mash it with a fork to desired consistency. Spread the mash onto each piece of toast.

3. Scatter the crumbled goat cheese on top and season as needed with salt. Serve immediately.

Healthy Chia Pudding

Prep Time: 5 minutes
Servings: 3-4

Recipe Ingredients:

- 4 cups of unsweetened almond milk
- ¾ cup of chia seeds
- 1 teaspoon of ground cinnamon
- Pinch sea salt

Cooking Instruction:

1. In a medium bowl, whisk together the almond milk, chia seeds, cinnamon, and sea salt until well incorporated.

2. Cover and transfer to the refrigerator to thicken for about 1 hour, or until a pudding-like texture is achieved. Serve chilled.

Banana-Blueberry Breakfast Cookies

Prep Time: 10 minutes
Cooking Time: 13 minutes
Servings: 4

Recipe Ingredients:

- 2 medium bananas, sliced
- 4 tablespoons of almond butter
- 4 large eggs, lightly beaten
- ½ cup of unsweetened applesauce
- 1 teaspoon of vanilla extract
- ⅔ cup of coconut flour
- ¼ teaspoon of salt
- 1 cup of fresh or frozen blueberries

Cooking Instruction:

1. First, preheat the oven to 375°F (190°C). Line a baking sheet with parchment paper.

2. Then, stir together the bananas and almond butter in a medium bowl until well incorporated.

3. Fold in the beaten eggs, applesauce, and vanilla and blend well. Add the coconut flour and salt and mix well. Add the blueberries and stir to just incorporate.

4. Drop about 2 tablespoons of dough onto the parchment paper-lined baking sheet for each cookie.

5. Using your clean hand, flatten each into a rounded biscuit shape, until it is 1 inch thick.

6. Bake in the preheated oven for about 13 minutes, or until the top is golden brown and a toothpick inserted in the center comes out clean. Let the cookies cool for 5 to 10 minutes before serving.

Blackberry-Yogurt Green Smoothie

Prep Time: 5 minutes
Servings: 1-2

Recipe Ingredients:

- 1 cup of plain Greek yogurt
- 1 cup of baby spinach
- ½ cup of frozen blackberries
- ½ cup of unsweetened almond milk
- ½ teaspoon of peeled and grated fresh ginger
- ¼ cup of chopped pecans

Cooking Instruction:

1. At first, process the yogurt, baby spinach, blackberries, almond milk, and ginger in a food processor until smoothly blended.

2. Divide the mixture into two bowls and serve topped with the chopped pecans.

Buckwheat Porridge

Prep Time: 5 minutes
Cooking Time: 40 minutes
Servings: 3-4

Recipe Ingredients:

- 3 cups of water
- 2 cups of raw buckwheat groats
- Pinch sea salt
- 1 cup of unsweetened almond milk

Cooking Instruction:

1. In a medium saucepan, add the water, buckwheat groats, and sea salt and bring to a boil over medium-high heat.

2. Once it starts to boil, reduce the heat to low. Cook for about 20 minutes, stirring occasionally, or until most of the water is absorbed.

3. Add the almond milk and whisk well. Continue cooking for about 15 minutes, or until the buckwheat groats are very softened. Ladle the porridge into bowls and serve warm.

Creamy Vanilla Oatmeal

Prep Time: 5 minutes
Cooking Time: 40 minutes
Servings: 3-4

Recipe Ingredients:

- 4 cups of water
- Pinch sea salt
- 1 cup of steel-cut oats
- ¾ cup of unsweetened almond milk
- 2 teaspoons of pure vanilla extract

Cooking Instruction:

1. Add the water and salt to a large saucepan over high heat and bring to a boil. Once boiling, reduce the heat to low and add the oats.

2. Mix well and cook for 30 minutes, stirring occasionally. Fold in the almond milk and vanilla and whisk to combine.

3. Continue cooking for about 10 minutes, or until the oats are thick and creamy. Ladle the oatmeal into bowls and serve warm.

White Beans with Greens & Poached Egg (Greek)

Prep Time: 10 minutes
Cooking Time: 0 minutes
Servings: 3-4

Recipe Ingredients:

- Za'atar: 2 teaspoons
- 3 tablespoons of olive oil
- 2 minced garlic cloves
- 1 teaspoon Kosher salt
- 4 eggs, poached
- 1 tablespoon Lemon juice
- 10 ounce of Swiss chard, stems removed & leaves sliced
- 1 can of (15-ounces) cannellini beans, rinsed
- ¼ teaspoon of Red pepper flakes

Cooking Instruction:

1. In a pan, add oil (2 tbsp.) on medium flame until hot. Add beans and cook for 2-4 minutes.

2. Add za'atar (1 teaspoon) and salt (half teaspoon), mix well. Cook for 3-5 minutes, until beans are golden brown, take them out on a plate.

3. Add oil (1 tbsp.) to the pan, add chard and season with the rest of the za'atar, salt, cook for 3-5 minutes.

4. Turn off the heat and add lemon juice and toss well. In four bowls, add beans and place a poached egg on top with red pepper flakes. Serve right away.

Salad with Spinach, Tomatoes, and Poached Egg (Italian)

Prep Time: 13 minutes
Cooking Time: 5 minutes
Servings: 1-2

Recipe Ingredients:

- 3 ounces of spinach
- 2 tomatoes
- 2 chicken egg
- 2 ounces of Feta cheese
- 1 tablespoon of vegetable oil
- 2 tablespoons of agave syrup
- 1 ½ teaspoons of sour cream 15%
- 2 teaspoons lemon juice
- 1 tablespoon of dill
- 1 ½ ounces of red onion
- Salt and pepper to taste

Cooking Instruction:

1. Pour the vegetable oil onto the cling film. Break the egg so that the yolk remains intact.

2. Then, collect the film with the egg in a bag, squeeze out the air, tie and cook for 5 minutes.

3. Mix the lemon juice, agave syrup (1 tablespoon), and vegetable oil, let the dressing rest.

4. Cut the tomatoes into a cube and the onion into strips, fill with salt and pepper dressing.

5. Add the spinach leaves, mix. Top with Feta cheese and poached egg. Mix the sour cream with the chopped dill and syrup (1 tbsp.). Pour over the salad dressing with the prepared sauce.

Potato Scallops with Truffle Oil (Spanish)

Prep Time: 8 minutes
Cooking Time: 24 minutes
Servings: 1-2

Recipe Ingredients

- 4 ounces of scallops
- 3 ounces of potato
- ½ ounce of Parmesan cheese
- ½ teaspoon of lime zest
- ½ ounce of butter
- 1 tablespoon of olive oil
- 1½ teaspoons of truffle oil
- 1 teaspoon of arugula
- 2/3 ounces of cherry tomatoes
- 1 chive
- ½ teaspoon of thyme Sea salt to taste
- Ground black pepper to taste

Cooking Instruction:

1. Start by frying the scallops on both sides in olive oil with thyme, salt, and pepper.

2. Then, boil the potatoes separately and rub them through a sieve. Add the zest of lime, grated Parmesan cheese, butter, salt, and pepper.

3. Lightly warm the arugula and cherry tomatoes in olive oil. Put the mashed potatoes through the ring on a plate, scallops symmetrically put on it, arugula and cherry on the scallops, garnish with the thyme and onion, and pour with the truffle oil.

Eggs and Salsa (Italian)

Prep Time: 5 minutes
Cooking Time: 5 minutes
Servings: 2

Recipe Ingredients

- 1 cup of tomatoes.
- 1 green onion (bunch).
- 1 bunch of cilantros, chopped.
- Juice from 1 lime.
- 1 cup red onion, chopped.
- 2 small habanero chilies, chopped.
- 8 eggs, whisked.
- Sea salt.
- A drizzle of olive oil.
- 2 garlic cloves, minced.

Cooking Instruction:

1. Mix tomatoes, green onions, red onion, habaneros, garlic, cilantro, and lime juice and toss well.

2. Add a pinch of salt, toss again and keep this in the fridge until you serve it. Heat up a pan with a drizzle of oil, add eggs, and scramble them for 4–5 minutes.

3. Divide scrambled eggs on plates, add salsa on top and serve.

Bacon & Cream Cheese Mug Muffins (Italian)

Prep Time: 15 minutes
Cooking Time: 15 minutes
Servings: 1-2

Recipe Ingredients:

- ¼ cup of flaxseed meal.
- 1 egg.
- 1 tablespoon of heavy cream.
- 2 tablespoons of pesto.
- ¼ cup of almond flour.
- ¼ teaspoon of baking soda.
- Salt and black pepper, to taste.
- 4 bacon slices.
- 2 tablespoons of cream cheese
- ½ medium avocado, sliced.

Cooking Instruction:

1. Mix the flaxseed meal, almond flour, and baking soda in a bowl. Add the egg, heavy cream, and pesto. Then whisk well. Season with salt and pepper.

2. Divide the mixture between 2 ramekins. Microwave for 60–90 seconds. Let cool slightly before filling.

3. Put the bacon in a nonstick skillet and cook until it becomes crispy, then set aside.

4. Transfer the muffins onto a plate and cut them in half crosswise. Assemble the sandwiches by spreading the cream cheese and topping with the bacon and avocado slices.

Crustless Tiropita (Greek Cheese Pie)

Prep Time: 10 minutes
Cooking Time: 35 to 40 mins
Servings: 5-6

Recipe Ingredients

- 4 tablespoons of extra-virgin olive oil, divided
- ½ cup of whole-milk ricotta cheese
- 1¼ cups of crumbled feta cheese
- 2 tablespoons of chopped fresh mint
- ½ teaspoon of lemon zest
- ¼ teaspoon of freshly ground black pepper
- 2 large eggs
- ½ teaspoon of baking powder
- 1 tablespoon of chopped fresh dill

Cooking Instruction:

1. Preheat the oven to 350°F (180°C). Coat the bottom and sides of a baking dish with 2 tablespoons of olive oil. Set aside.

2. Mix together the ricotta and feta cheese in a medium bowl and stir with a fork until well combined. Add the dill, mint, lemon zest, and black pepper and mix well.

3. In a separate bowl, whisk together the eggs and baking powder. Pour the whisked eggs into the bowl of cheese mixture. Blend well.

4. Slowly pour the mixture into the coated baking dish and drizzle with the remaining 2 tablespoons of olive oil.

5. Bake in the preheated oven for about 35 to 40 minutes, or until the pie is browned around the edges and cooked through. Cool for 5 minutes before slicing into wedges.

Fluffy Almond Flour Pancakes with Strawberries

Prep Time: 5 minutes
Cooking Time: 15 minutes
Servings: 3-4

Recipe Ingredients

- 1 cup of plus 2 tablespoons unsweetened almond milk
- 1 cup almond flour
- 2 large eggs, whisked ⅓ cup honey
- 1 teaspoon of baking soda
- ¼ teaspoon of salt
- 2 tablespoons of extra-virgin olive oil
- 1 cup of sliced strawberries

Cooking Instruction:

1. Combine the almond milk, almond flour, whisked eggs, honey, baking soda, and salt in a large bowl and whisk to incorporate.

2. Heat the olive oil in a large skillet over medium-high heat. Make the pancakes: Pour ⅓ cup of batter into the hot skillet and swirl the pan so the batter covers the bottom evenly.

3. Next, cook for 2 to 3 minutes until the pancake turns golden brown around the edges.

4. Flip the pancake with a spatula and cook for 2 to 3 minutes until cooked through. Repeat with the remaining batter.

5. Serve the pancakes with the sliced strawberries on top.

Chapter 2: Side Salad and soup Recipe

Grilled Bell Pepper and Anchovy Antipasto

Prep Time: 15 minutes
Cooking Time: 8 minutes
Servings: 4

Recipe Ingredients:

- 2 tablespoons of extra-virgin olive oil, divided
- 4 medium red bell peppers, quartered, stem and seeds removed
- 6 ounces (170 g) anchovies in oil, chopped
- 2 tablespoons of capers, rinsed and drained
- 1 cup of Kalamata olives, pitted
- 1 small shallot, chopped
- Sea salt and freshly ground pepper, to taste

Cooking Instruction:

1. Heat the grill to medium-high heat. Grease the grill grates with 1 tablespoon of olive oil.

2. Arrange the red bell peppers on the preheated grill grates, then grill for 8 minutes or until charred.

3. Turn off the grill and allow the pepper to cool for 10 minutes. Transfer the charred pepper in a colander.

4. Rinse and peel the peppers under running cold water, then pat dry with paper towels.

5. Cut the peppers into chunks and combine with remaining in a large bowl. Toss to mix well. Serve immediately.

Marinated Mushrooms and Olives

Prep Time: 1 hour 10 minutes
Cooking Time: 0 minutes
Servings: 7-8

Recipe Ingredients:

- 1 pound (454 g) white button mushrooms, rinsed and drained
- 1 pound (454 g) fresh olives
- ½ tablespoon of crushed fennel seeds
- 1 tablespoon of white wine vinegar
- 2 tablespoons of fresh thyme leaves
- Pinch chili flakes
- Sea salt and freshly ground pepper, to taste
- 2 tablespoons of extra-virgin olive oil

Cooking Instruction:

1. Combine all in a large bowl. Toss to mix well. Wrap the bowl in plastic and refrigerate for at least 1 hour to marinate.

2. Remove the bowl from the refrigerate and let sit under room temperature for 10 minutes, then serve.

Root Vegetable Roast

Prep Time: 15 minutes
Cooking Time: 25 minutes
Servings: 4 to 6

Recipe Ingredients:

- 1 bunch beets, peeled and cut into 1-inch cubes
- 2 small sweet potatoes, peeled and cut into 1-inch cubes
- 3 parsnips, peeled and cut into 1-inch rounds
- 4 carrots, peeled and cut into 1-inch rounds
- 1 tablespoon of raw honey
- 1 teaspoon of sea salt
- ½ teaspoon of freshly ground black pepper
- 1 tablespoon of extra-virgin olive oil
- 2 tablespoons of coconut oil, melted

Cooking Instruction:

1. Preheat the oven to 400°F (205°C). Line a baking sheet with parchment paper. Combine all in a large bowl. Toss to coat the vegetables well.

2. Next, pour the mixture in the baking sheet, then place the sheet in the preheated oven.

3. Roast for 25 minutes or until the vegetables are lightly browned and soft. Flip the vegetables halfway through the cooking time.

4. Remove the vegetables from the oven and allow to cool before serving.

Arugula and Fig Salad

Prep Time: 15 minutes
Cooking Time: 0 minutes
Servings: 2

Recipe Ingredients:

- 3 cups arugula
- 4 fresh, ripe figs (or 4 to 6 dried figs), stemmed and sliced
- 2 tablespoons of olive oil
- ¼ cup of lightly toasted pecan halves
- 2 tablespoons of crumbled blue cheese
- 1 to 2 tablespoons of balsamic glaze

Cooking Instruction:

1. Toss the arugula and figs with the olive oil in a large bowl until evenly coated. Add the pecans and blue cheese to the bowl.

2. Toss the salad lightly. Drizzle with the balsamic glaze and serve immediately.

Sardines with Lemony Tomato Sauce

Prep Time: 10 minutes
Cooking Time: 40 minutes
Servings: 4

Recipe Ingredients:

- 2 tablespoons of olive oil, divided
- 4 Roma tomatoes, peeled and chopped, reserve the juice
- 1 small onion, sliced thinly
- Zest of 1 orange
- Sea salt and freshly ground pepper, to taste
- 1 pound of (454 g) fresh sardines, rinsed, spine removed, butterflied
- ½ cup of white wine
- 2 tablespoons of whole-wheat breadcrumbs

Cooking Instruction:

1. Preheat the oven to 425°F (220°C). Grease a baking dish with 1 tablespoon of olive oil.

2. Heat the remaining olive oil in a nonstick skillet over medium-low heat until shimmering.

3. Add the tomatoes with juice, onion, orange zest, salt, and ground pepper to the skillet and simmer for 20 minutes or until it thickens.

4. Pour half of the mixture on the bottom of the baking dish, then top with the butterflied sardines.

5. Also pour the remaining mixture and white wine over the sardines. Spread the breadcrumbs on top, then place the baking dish in the preheated oven.

6. Bake for 20 minutes or until the fish is opaque. Remove the baking sheet from the oven and serve the sardines warm.

Garlic Wilted Greens

Prep Time: 10 minutes
Cooking Time: 5 minutes
Servings: 1-2

Recipe Ingredients:

- 1 tablespoon of olive oil
- 2 garlic cloves, minced
- 3 cups of sliced greens (spinach, chard, beet greens, dandelion greens, or a combination) Pinch salt
- Pinch red pepper flakes (or more to taste)

Cooking Instruction:

1. At first, heat the olive oil in a skillet over medium-high heat. Add garlic and sauté for 30 seconds, or just until fragrant.

2. Add the greens, salt, and pepper flakes and stir to combine. Let the greens wilt, but do not overcook. Remove from the skillet and serve on a plate.

Greens, Fennel, and Pear Soup with Cashews

Prep Time: 15 minutes
Cooking Time: 15 minutes
Servings: 4 to 6

Recipe Ingredients:

- 2 tablespoons of olive oil
- 1 fennel bulb, cut into ¼-inch-thick slices
- 2 leeks, white part only, sliced
- 2 pears, peeled, cored, and cut into ½-inch cubes
- 1 teaspoon of sea salt
- ¼ teaspoon of freshly ground black pepper
- ½ cup cashews
- 2 cups of packed blanched spinach
- 3 cups of low-sodium vegetable soup

Cooking Instruction:

1. To begin, heat the olive oil in a stockpot over high heat until shimmering. Add the fennel and leeks, then sauté for 5 minutes or until tender.

2. Add the pears and sprinkle with salt and pepper, then sauté for another 3 minutes or until the pears are soft.

3. Add the cashews, spinach, and vegetable soup. Bring to a boil. Reduce the heat to low. Cover and simmer for 5 minutes.

4. Pour the soup in a food processor, then pulse until creamy and smooth. Pour the soup back to the pot and heat over low heat until heated through.

5. Transfer the soup to a large serving bowl and serve immediately.

Veggie Slaw

Prep Time: 20 minutes
Cooking Time: 0 minutes
Servings: 4 to 6

Recipe Ingredients:
Salad:

- 2 large broccoli stems, peeled and shredded
- ½ celery root bulb, peeled and shredded
- ¼ cup of chopped fresh Italian parsley
- 1 large beet, peeled and shredded
- 2 carrots, peeled and shredded
- 1 small red onion, sliced thin

Dressing:

- 1 teaspoon of Dijon mustard
- ½ cup of apple cider vinegar
- 1 tablespoon of raw honey
- 1 teaspoon of sea salt
- ¼ teaspoon of freshly ground black pepper
- 2 tablespoons of extra-virgin olive oil

Topping:

- ½ cup of crumbled feta cheese
- 2 zucchinis, shredded

Cooking Instruction:

1. Combine the Ingredients for the salad in a large salad bowl, then toss to combine well.

2. Combine the items for the dressing in a small bowl, then stir to mix well. Dress the salad, then serve with feta cheese on top.

Rich Chicken and Small Pasta Broth

Prep Time: 10 minutes
Cooking Time: 4 hours
Servings: 6

Recipe Ingredients:

- 6 boneless, skinless chicken thighs
- 4 stalks celery, cut into
- ½-inch pieces
- 4 carrots, cut into 1-inch pieces
- 1 medium yellow onion, halved
- 2 garlic cloves, minced
- 2 bay leaves
- Sea salt and freshly ground black pepper, to taste
- 6 cups of low-sodium chicken stock
- ½ cup of stelline pasta
- ¼ cup of chopped fresh flat-leaf parsley

Cooking Instruction:

1. To begin, combine the chicken thighs, celery, carrots, onion, and garlic in the slow cooker.

2. Spread with bay leaves and sprinkle with salt and pepper. Toss to mix well. Pour in the chicken stock.

3. Put the lid on and cook on high for 4 hours or until the internal temperature of chicken reaches at least 165°F (74°C).

4. In the last 20 minutes of the cooking, remove the chicken from the slow cooker and transfer to a bowl to cool until ready to reserve.

5. Discard the bay leaves and add the pasta to the slow cooker. Put the lid on and cook for 15 minutes or until al dente.

6. Meanwhile, slice the chicken, then put the chicken and parsley in the slow cooker and cook for 5 minutes or until well combined.

7. Pour the soup in a large bowl and serve immediately.

Lemon and Spinach Orzo

Prep Time: 5 minutes
Cooking Time: 10 minutes
Serve: Makes 2 cups

Recipe Ingredients:

- 1 cup of dry orzo
- 1 (6-ounce / 170-g) bag baby spinach
- 1 cup of halved grape tomatoes
- 2 tablespoons of extra-virgin olive oil
- ¼ teaspoon of salt
- Freshly ground black pepper
- ¾ cup of crumbled feta cheese
- 1 lemon, juiced and zested

Cooking Instruction:

1. To begin, bring a medium pot of water to a boil. Stir in the orzo and cook uncovered for 8 minutes.

2. Drain the water, then return the orzo to medium heat. Add the spinach and tomatoes and cook until the spinach is wilted.

3. Sprinkle with the olive oil, salt, and pepper and mix well. Top with the feta cheese, lemon juice and zest, then toss one or two more times and serve.

Mixed Salad with Balsamic Honey Dressing

Prep Time: 15 minutes
Servings: 2

Recipe Ingredients:
Dressing:

- ¼ cup of balsamic vinegar
- ¼ cup of olive oil
- 1 tablespoon of honey
- 1 teaspoon of Dijon mustard
- ¼ teaspoon of garlic powder
- ¼ teaspoon of salt, or more to taste
- Pinch freshly ground black pepper

Salad:

- ½ cup of cherry or grape tomatoes, halved
- ½ English cucumber, sliced in quarters lengthwise and then cut into bite-size pieces
- Any combination fresh, torn herbs (parsley, oregano, basil, or chives)
- 1 tablespoon of roasted sunflower seeds
- 4 cups of chopped red leaf lettuce

Cooking Instruction:
To Make the Dressing

1. Combine the vinegar, olive oil, honey, mustard, garlic powder, salt, and pepper in a jar with a lid. Shake well.

Make the Salad:

2. In a large bowl, combine the lettuce, tomatoes, cucumber, and herbs and toss well.

3. Pour all or as much dressing as desired over the tossed salad and toss again to coat the salad with dressing. Top with the sunflower seeds before serving.

Orange-Honey Glazed Carrots

Prep Time: 10 minutes
Cooking Time: 15 to 20 minutes
Servings: 2

Recipe Ingredients:

- ½ pound of (227 g) rainbow carrots, peeled
- 2 tablespoons of fresh orange juice
- 1 tablespoon of honey
- ½ teaspoon of coriander
- Pinch salt

Cooking Instruction:

1. Preheat the oven to 400°F (205°C). Cut the carrots lengthwise into slices of even thickness and place in a large bowl.

2. Stir together the orange juice, honey, coriander, and salt in a small bowl. Pour the orange juice mixture over the carrots and toss until well coated.

3. Spread the carrots in a baking dish in a single layer. Roast for 15 to 20 minutes until fork-tender. Let cool for 5 minutes before serving.

Moroccan Lentil, Tomato, and Cauliflower Soup

Prep Time: 15 minutes
Cooking Time: 4 hours
Servings: 5-6

Recipe Ingredients:

- 1 cup of chopped carrots
- 1 cup of chopped onions
- 3 cloves garlic, minced
- ½ teaspoon of ground coriander
- 1 teaspoon of ground cumin
- 1 teaspoon of ground turmeric
- ¼ teaspoon of ground cinnamon
- ¼ teaspoon of freshly ground black pepper
- 1 cup of dry lentils
- 1 tablespoon of red wine vinegar (optional)
- 28 ounces of (794 g) tomatoes, diced, reserve the juice
- 1½ cups of chopped cauliflower
- 4 cups of low-sodium vegetable soup
- 1 tablespoon of no-salt-added tomato paste
- 1 teaspoon of extra-virgin olive oil
- 1 cup of chopped fresh spinach
- ¼ cup of chopped fresh cilantro

Cooking Instruction:

1. Put the carrots and onions in the slow cooker, then sprinkle with minced garlic, coriander, cumin, turmeric, cinnamon, and black pepper. Stir to combine well.

2. Add the lentils, tomatoes, and cauliflower, then pour in the vegetable soup and tomato paste.

3. Drizzle with olive oil. Stir to combine well. Put the slow cooker lid on and cook on high for 4 hours or until the vegetables are tender.

4. In the last 30 minutes during the cooking time, open the lid and stir the soup, then fold in the spinach.

5. Pour the cooked soup in a large serving bowl, then spread with cilantro and drizzle with vinegar. Serve immediately.

Tricolor Summer Salad

Prep Time: 10 minutes
Servings: 3 to 4

Recipe Ingredients:

- ¼ cup of while balsamic vinegar
- 2 tablespoons of Dijon mustard
- 1 tablespoon of sugar
- ½ teaspoon of garlic salt
- ½ teaspoon of freshly ground black pepper
- ¼ cup of extra-virgin olive oil
- 1½ cups of chopped orange, yellow, and red tomatoes
- ½ cucumber, peeled and diced
- 1 small red onion, thinly sliced
- ¼ cup of crumbled feta (optional)

Cooking Instruction:

1. In a small bowl, whisk the vinegar, mustard, sugar, pepper, and garlic salt. Then slowly whisk in the olive oil.

2. In a large bowl, add the tomatoes, cucumber, and red onion. Add the dressing. Toss once or twice, and serve with the feta crumbles (if desired) sprinkled on top.

Mushroom and Soba Noodle Soup

Prep Time: 15 minutes
Cooking Time: 10 minutes
Servings: 3-4

Recipe Ingredients:

- 2 tablespoons of coconut oil
- 8 ounces (227 g) shiitake mushrooms, stemmed and sliced thin
- 1 tablespoon of minced fresh ginger
- 4 scallions, sliced thin
- 1 garlic clove, minced
- 1 teaspoon of sea salt
- 4 cups of low-sodium vegetable broth
- 3 cups of water
- 4 ounces of (113 g) soba noodles
- 1 bunch spinach, blanched, rinsed and cut into strips
- 1 tablespoon of freshly squeezed lemon juice

Cooking Instruction:

1. Heat the coconut oil in a stockpot over medium heat until melted. Add the mushrooms, ginger, scallions, garlic, and salt. Sauté for 5 minutes or until fragrant and the mushrooms are tender.

2. Pour in the vegetable broth and water. Bring to a boil, then add the soba noodles and cook for 5 minutes or until al dente.

3. Turn off the heat and add the spinach and lemon juice. Stir to mix well. Pour the soup in a large bowl and serve immediately.

Parmesan Roasted Red Potatoes

Prep Time: 10 minutes
Cooking Time: 55 minutes
Servings: 1-2

Recipe Ingredients:

- 12 ounces (340g) red potatoes (3 to 4 small potatoes), scrubbed and diced into 1-inch pieces
- 1 tablespoon of olive oil
- ½ teaspoon of garlic powder
- ¼ teaspoon salt
- 1 tablespoon of grated Parmesan cheese
- 1 teaspoon of minced fresh rosemary (from 1 sprig)

Cooking Instruction:

1. Preheat the oven to 425°F (220°C). Once preheated, line a baking sheet with parchment paper.

2. In a mixing bowl, combine the potatoes, olive oil, garlic powder, and salt. Toss well to coat. Lay the potatoes on the parchment paper and roast for 10 minutes.

3. Flip the potatoes over and roast for another 10 minutes. Check the potatoes to make sure they are golden brown on the top and bottom.

4. Toss them again, turn the heat down to 350°F (180°C), and roast for 30 minutes more.

5. When the potatoes are golden brown, scatter the Parmesan cheese over them and toss again. Return to the oven for 3 minutes to melt the cheese.

6. Remove from the oven and sprinkle with the fresh rosemary before serving.

Chapter 3: Sandwiches Recipes, Pizzas Recipes, & Wraps Recipes

Pizza Pockets

Prep Time: 10 minutes
Servings: 1-2

Recipe Ingredients:

- ½ cup of tomato sauce
- ½ teaspoon of oregano
- ½ teaspoon of garlic powder
- ½ cup of chopped black olives
- 2 canned artichoke hearts, drained and chopped
- 2 ounces of (57 g) pepperoni, chopped
- ½ cup of shredded Mozzarella cheese
- 1 whole-wheat pita, halved

Cooking Instruction:

1. In a medium bowl, stir together the tomato sauce, oregano, and garlic powder. Add the olives, artichoke hearts, pepperoni, and cheese. Stir to mix.

2. Spoon the mixture into the pita halves and serve.

Grilled Caesar Salad Sandwiches

Prep Time: 5 minutes
Cooking Time: 5 minutes
Servings: 2

Recipe Ingredients:

- ¾ cup of olive oil, divided
- 2 romaine lettuce hearts, left intact
- 3 to 4 anchovy fillets
- Juice of 1 lemon
- 2 to 3 cloves garlic, peeled
- 1 teaspoon of Dijon mustard
- ¼ teaspoon of Worcestershire sauce
- Sea salt and freshly ground pepper, to taste
- 2 slices whole-wheat bread, toasted
- Freshly grated Parmesan cheese, for serving

Cooking Instruction:

1. To begin, preheat the grill to medium-high heat and oil the grates. On a cutting board, drizzle the lettuce with 1 to 2 tablespoons of olive oil and place on the grates.

2. Grill for 5 minutes, turning until lettuce is slightly charred on all sides. Let lettuce cool enough to handle.

3. In a food processor, combine the remaining olive oil with the anchovies, lemon juice, garlic, mustard, and Worcestershire sauce.

4. Pulse the until you have a smooth emulsion. Season with sea salt and freshly ground pepper to taste. Chop the lettuce in half and place on the bread.

5. Drizzle with the dressing and serve with a sprinkle of Parmesan cheese.

Chickpea Lettuce Wraps

Prep Time: 15 minutes
Servings: 1-2

Recipe Ingredients:

- 1 (15-ounce / 425-g) can chickpeas, drained and rinsed well
- 1 celery stalk, diced
- ½ shallot, minced
- 1 green apple, cored and diced
- 3 tablespoons of tahini (sesame paste)
- 2 teaspoons of freshly squeezed lemon juice
- 1 teaspoon of raw honey
- 1 teaspoon of Dijon mustard Dash salt
- Filtered water, to thin
- 4 romaine lettuce leaves

Cooking Instruction:

1. In a medium bowl, stir together the chickpeas, celery, shallot, apple, tahini, lemon juice, honey, mustard, and salt.

2. If needed, add some water to thin the mixture. Place the romaine lettuce leaves on a plate.

3. Fill each with the chickpea filling, using it all. Wrap the leaves around the filling. Serve immediately.

Mashed Grape Tomato Pizzas

Prep Time: 10 minutes
Cooking Time: 20 minutes
Servings: 5-6

Recipe Ingredients:

- 3 cups of grape tomatoes, halved
- 1 teaspoon of chopped fresh thyme leaves
- 2 garlic cloves, minced
- ¼ teaspoon of kosher salt ¼ teaspoon freshly ground black pepper
- 1 tablespoon of extra-virgin olive oil
- ¾ cup of shredded Parmesan cheese
- 6 whole-wheat pita breads

Cooking Instruction:

1. At first, preheat the oven to 425°F (220°C). Combine the tomatoes, thyme, garlic, salt, ground black pepper, and olive oil in a baking pan.

2. Roast in the preheated oven for 20 minutes. Remove the pan from the oven, mash the tomatoes with a spatula and stir to mix well halfway through the cooking time.

3. Meanwhile, divide and spread the cheese over each pita bread, then place the bread in a separate baking pan and roast in the oven for 5 minutes or until golden brown and the cheese melts.

4. Transfer the pita bread onto a large plate, then top with the roasted mashed tomatoes. Serve immediately.

Dulse, Avocado, and Tomato Pitas

Prep Time: 10 minutes
Cooking Time: 30 minutes
Servings: Makes 4 pitas

Recipe Ingredients:

- 2 teaspoons of coconut oil
- ½ cup of dulse, picked through and separated
- Ground black pepper, to taste
- 2 avocados, sliced
- 2 tablespoons of lime juice
- ¼ cup of chopped cilantro 2 scallions, white and light green parts, sliced
- Sea salt, to taste
- 4 (8-inch) whole wheat pitas, sliced in half
- 4 cups of chopped romaine
- 4 plum tomatoes, sliced

Cooking Instruction:

1. Heat the coconut oil in a nonstick skillet over medium heat until melted. Add the dulse and sauté for 5 minutes or until crispy.

2. Sprinkle with ground black pepper and turn off the heat. Set aside. Put the avocado, lime juice, cilantro, and scallions in a food processor and sprinkle with salt and ground black pepper. Pulse to combine well until smooth.

3. Toast the pitas in a baking pan in the oven for 1 minute until soft. Transfer the pitas to a clean work surface and open.

4. Spread the avocado mixture over the pitas, then top with dulse, romaine, and tomato slices. Serve immediately.

Vegetable and Cheese Lavash Pizza

Prep Time: 15 minutes
Cooking Time: 11 minutes
Servings: 3-4

Recipe Ingredients:

- 2 (12 by 9-inch) lavash breads
- 2 tablespoons of extra-virgin olive oil
- 10 ounces of (284 g) frozen spinach, thawed and squeezed dry
- 1 cup of shredded fontina cheese
- 1 tomato, cored and cut into ½-inch pieces
- ½ cup of pitted large green olives, chopped
- ¼ teaspoon of red pepper flakes
- 3 garlic cloves, minced
- ¼ teaspoon of sea salt
- ¼ teaspoon of ground black pepper
- ½ cup of grated Parmesan cheese

Cooking Instruction:

1. Preheat oven to 475°F (246°C). Once the oven is preheated, brush the lavash breads with olive oil, then place them on two baking sheets.

2. Heat in the preheated oven for 4 minutes or until lightly browned. Flip the breads halfway through the cooking time.

3. Meanwhile, combine the spinach, fontina cheese, tomato pieces, olives, red pepper flakes, garlic, salt, and black pepper in a large bowl. Stir to mix well.

4. Remove the lavash bread from the oven and sit them on two large plates, spread them with the spinach mixture, then scatter with the Parmesan cheese on top.

5. Bake in the oven for 7 minutes or until the cheese melts and well browned. Slice and serve warm.

Greek Vegetable Salad Pita

Prep Time: 10 minutes
Servings: 3-4

Recipe Ingredients:

- ½ cup of baby spinach leaves
- ½ small red onion, thinly sliced
- ½ small cucumber, deseeded and chopped
- 1 tomato, chopped
- 1 cup of chopped romaine lettuce
- 1 tablespoon of extra-virgin olive oil
- ½ tablespoon of red wine vinegar
- 1 teaspoon of Dijon mustard
- 1 tablespoon of crumbled feta cheese
- Sea salt and freshly ground pepper, to taste
- 1 whole-wheat pita

Cooking Instruction:

1. Combine all the Ingredients except for the pita, in a large bowl. Toss to mix well. Stuff the pita with the salad, then serve immediately.

Falafel Balls with Tahini Sauce

Prep Time: 2 hours 20 minutes
Cooking Time: 20 minutes
Servings: 3-4

Recipe Ingredients:
Tahini Sauce:

- ½ cup of tahini
- 2 tablespoons of lemon juice
- ¼ cup of finely chopped flat-leaf parsley
- 2 cloves garlic, minced
- ½ cup of cold water, as needed

Falafel:

- 1 cup of dried chickpeas, soaked overnight, drained
- ¼ cup of chopped flat-leaf parsley
- ¼ cup of chopped cilantro
- 1 large onion, chopped
- 1 teaspoon of cumin
- ½ teaspoon of chili flakes
- 4 cloves garlic
- 1 teaspoon of sea salt
- 5 tablespoons of almond flour
- 1½ teaspoons of baking soda, dissolved in 1 teaspoon water
- 2 cups of peanut oil
- 1 medium bell pepper, chopped
- 1 medium tomato, chopped
- 4 whole-wheat pita breads

Cooking Instruction:

Make the Tahini Sauce

1 Combine ingredients for the tahini sauce in a small bowl. Stir to mix well until smooth. Wrap the bowl in plastic and refrigerate until ready to serve.

Make the Falafel

2 Put the chickpeas, parsley, cilantro, onion, cumin, chili flakes, garlic, and salt in a food processor. Pulse to mix well but not puréed.

3 Add the flour and baking soda to the food processor, then pulse to form a smooth and tight dough.

4 Put the dough in a large bowl and wrap in plastic. Refrigerate for at least 2 hours to let it rise.

5 Divide and shape the dough into walnut-sized small balls. Pour the peanut oil in a large pot and heat over high heat until the temperature of the oil reaches 375°F (190°C).

6 Drop 6 balls into the oil each time, and fry for 5 minutes or until golden brown and crispy.

7 Turn the balls with a strainer to make them fried evenly. Transfer the balls on paper towels with the strainer, then drain the oil from the balls.

8 Roast the pita breads in the oven for 5 minutes or until golden brown, if needed, then stuff the pitas with falafel balls and top with bell peppers and tomatoes. Drizzle with tahini sauce and serve immediately.

Glazed Mushroom and Vegetable Fajitas

Prep Time: 20 minutes
Cooking Time: 20 minutes
Servings: 5-6

Recipe Ingredients:

- Spicy Glazed Mushrooms:
- 1 teaspoon of olive oil
- 1 (10- to 12-ounce / 284- to 340-g) package cremini mushrooms, rinsed and drained, cut into thin slices
- 1 teaspoon of chili powder
- Sea salt and freshly ground black pepper, to taste
- 1 teaspoon of maple syrup

Fajitas:

- 2 teaspoons of olive oil
- 1 onion, chopped
- Sea salt, to taste
- 1 bell pepper, any color, deseeded and sliced into long strips
- 1 zucchini, cut into large matchsticks
- 6 whole-grain tortilla
- 2 carrots, grated
- 3 to 4 scallions, sliced
- ½ cup of fresh cilantro, finely chopped

Cooking Instruction:

Make the Spicy Glazed Mushrooms

1. Heat the olive oil in a nonstick skillet over medium heat until shimmering. Add the mushrooms and sauté for 10 minutes or until tender.

2. Sprinkle the mushrooms with chili powder, salt, and ground black pepper. Drizzle with maple syrup.

3. Stir to mix well and cook for 5 to 7 minutes or until the mushrooms are glazed. Set aside until ready to use.

Make the Fajitas

1. Heat the olive oil in the same skillet over medium heat until shimmering. Add the onion and sauté for 5 minutes or until translucent. Sprinkle with salt.

2. Add the bell pepper and zucchini and sauté for 7 minutes or until tender. Meanwhile, toast the tortilla in the oven for 5 minutes or until golden brown.

3. Allow the tortilla to cool for a few minutes until they can be handled, then assemble the tortilla with glazed mushrooms, sautéed vegetables and remaining vegetables to make the fajitas. Serve immediately.

Green Veggie Sandwiches

Prep Time: 20 minutes
Servings: 1-2

Recipe Ingredients:
Spread:

- 1 (15-ounce / 425-g) can cannellini beans, drained and rinsed
- ⅓ cup of packed fresh basil leaves
- ⅓ cup of packed fresh parsley
- ⅓ cup of chopped fresh chives
- 2 garlic cloves, chopped
- Zest and juice of ½ lemon
- 1 tablespoon of apple cider vinegar

Sandwiches:

- 4 whole-grain bread slices, toasted
- 8 English cucumber slices
- 1 large beefsteak tomato, cut into slices
- 1 large avocado, halved, pitted, and cut into slices
- 1 small yellow bell pepper, cut into slices
- 2 handfuls broccoli sprouts
- 2 handfuls fresh spinach

Cooking Instruction:

Make the Spread

1. In a food processor, combine the cannellini beans, basil, parsley, chives, garlic, lemon zest and juice, and vinegar.

2. Pulse a few times, scrape down the sides, and purée until smooth. You may need to scrape down the sides again to incorporate all the basil and parsley.

3. Refrigerate for at least 1 hour to allow the flavors to blend. Assemble the Sandwiches.

4. Build your sandwiches by spreading several tablespoons of spread on each slice of bread.

5. Layer two slices of bread with the cucumber, tomato, avocado, bell pepper, broccoli sprouts, and spinach.

6. Top with the remaining bread slices and press down lightly. Serve immediately.

Mushroom-Pesto Baked Pizza

Prep Time: 5 minutes
Cooking Time: 15 minutes
Servings: 1-2

Recipe Ingredients:

- 1 teaspoon of extra-virgin olive oil
- ½ cup of sliced mushrooms
- ½ red onion, sliced
- Salt and freshly ground black pepper
- ¼ cup of store-bought pesto sauce
- 2 whole-wheat flatbreads
- ¼ cup of shredded Mozzarella cheese

Cooking Instruction:

1 At first, preheat the oven to 350°F (180°C). In a small skillet, heat the oil over medium heat.

2 Add the mushrooms and onion, and season with salt and pepper. Sauté for 3 to 5 minutes until the onion and mushrooms begin to soften.

3 Spread 2 tablespoons of pesto on each flatbread. Divide the mushroom-onion mixture between the two flatbreads.

4 Top each with 2 tablespoons of cheese. Place the flatbreads on a baking sheet and bake for 10 to 12 minutes until the cheese is melted and bubbly. Serve warm.

Tuna and Hummus Wraps

Prep Time: 10 minutes
Servings: 1-2

Recipe Ingredients:
Hummus:

- 1 cup of from 1 (15-ounce / 425-g) can low-sodium chickpeas, drained and rinsed
- 2 tablespoons of tahini
- 1 tablespoon of extra-virgin olive oil
- 1 garlic clove
- Juice of ½ lemon
- 2 tablespoons water

Wraps:

- 4 large lettuce leaves
- 1 (5-ounce / 142-g) can chunk light tuna packed in water, drained
- 1 red bell pepper, seeded and cut into strips
- 1 cucumber, sliced
- ¼ teaspoon of salt

Cooking Instruction:
Make the Hummus

1. In a blender jar, combine the chickpeas, tahini, olive oil, garlic, lemon juice, salt, and water.

2. Process until smooth. Taste and adjust with additional lemon juice or salt, as needed.

Make the Wraps

1. On each lettuce leaf, spread 1 tablespoon of hummus, and divide the tuna among the leaves.

2. Top each with several strips of red pepper and cucumber slices. Roll up the lettuce leaves, folding in the two shorter sides and rolling away from you, like a burrito.

Tuna and Olive Salad Sandwiches

Prep Time: 10 minutes
Servings: 3-4

Recipe Ingredients:

- 3 tablespoons of freshly squeezed lemon juice
- 2 tablespoons of extra-virgin olive oil
- 1 garlic clove, minced
- ½ teaspoon of freshly ground black pepper
- 2 (5-ounce / 142-g) cans tuna, drained
- 1 (2.25-ounce / 64-g) can sliced olives, any green or black variety
- ½ cup of chopped fresh fennel, including fronds
- 8 slices whole-grain crusty bread

Cooking Instruction:

1 In a medium bowl, whisk together the lemon juice, oil, garlic, and pepper. Add the tuna, olives and fennel to the bowl.

2 Using a fork, separate the tuna into chunks and stir to incorporate all the. Divide the tuna salad equally among 4 slices of bread.

3 Top each with the remaining bread slices. Let the sandwiches sit for at least 5 minutes so the zesty filling can soak into the bread before serving.

Mediterranean Greek Salad Wraps

Prep Time: 15 minutes
Servings: 3-4

Recipe Ingredients:

- 1½ cups of seedless cucumber, peeled and chopped
- 1 cup of chopped tomato
- ½ cup of finely chopped fresh mint
- ¼ cup of diced red onion
- 1 (2.25-ounce / 64-g) can sliced black olives, drained
- 2 tablespoons of extra-virgin olive oil 1 tablespoon red wine vinegar
- ¼ teaspoon of kosher salt
- ¼ teaspoon of freshly ground black pepper
- ½ cup of crumbled goat cheese
- 4 whole-wheat flatbread wraps or soft whole-wheat tortillas

Cooking Instruction:

1 In a large bowl, stir together the cucumber, tomato, mint, onion and olives. In a small bowl, whisk together the oil, vinegar, salt, and pepper.

2 Spread the dressing over the salad. Toss gently to combine. On a clean work surface, lay the wraps.

3 Divide the goat cheese evenly among the wraps. Scoop a quarter of the salad filling down the center of each wrap.

4 Fold up each wrap: Start by folding up the bottom, then fold one side over and fold the other side over the top. Repeat with the remaining wraps.

Chapter 4: Beans Recipes, Grains Recipes, & Pastas Recipes

Super Cheesy Tagliatelle

Prep Time: 10 minutes
Cooking Time: 20 minutes
Servings: 5-6

Recipe Ingredients:

- ¼ cup of goat cheese, chevre
- ¼ cup of grated Pecorino cheese
- ½ cup of grated Parmesan
- 1 cup of heavy cream
- ½ cup of grated Gouda
- 2 tablespoons of olive oil
- 1 tablespoon of Italian Seasoning mix
- 1 cup of vegetable broth
- 1 pound of (454 g) tagliatelle

Cooking Instruction:

1. In a bowl, mix goat cheese, pecorino, Parmesan, and heavy cream. Stir in Italian seasoning. Transfer to your instant pot. Stir in the broth and olive oil.

2. Seal the lid and cook on High Pressure for 4 minutes. Do a quick release. Meanwhile, drop the tagliatelle in boiling water and cook for 6 minutes.

3. Remove the instant pot's lid and stir in the tagliatelle. Top with grated gouda and let simmer for about 10 minutes on Sauté mode.

Chickpea Curry

Prep Time: 10 minutes
Cooking Time: 24 minutes
Servings: 3-4

Recipe Ingredients:

- ½ cup of raw chickpeas
- 1½ tablespoons of cooking oil
- ½ cup of chopped onions
- 1 bay leaf
- ½ tablespoon of grated garlic
- ¼ tablespoon of grated ginger
- ¾ cup of water
- 1 cup of fresh tomato purée
- ½ green chili, finely chopped
- ¼ teaspoon of turmeric
- ½ teaspoon of coriander powder
- 1 teaspoon of chili powder
- 1 cup of chopped baby spinach
- Salt, to taste
- Boiled white rice, for serving

Cooking Instruction:

1. Add the oil and onions to the Instant Pot. Sauté for 5 minutes. Stir in ginger, garlic paste, green chili and bay leaf. Cook for 1 minute, then add all the spices.

2. Add the chickpeas, tomato purée and the water to the pot. Cover and secure the lid.

3. Turn its pressure release handle to the sealing position. Cook on the Manual function with High Pressure for 15 mins.

4. After the beep, do a Natural release for 20 minutes. Stir in spinach and cook for 3 minutes on the Sauté setting. Serve hot with boiled white rice.

Cumin Quinoa Pilaf

Prep Time: 5 minutes
Cooking Time: 5 minutes
Servings: 1-2

Recipe Ingredients:

- 2 tablespoons of extra virgin olive oil
- 2 cloves garlic, minced
- 3 cups of water
- 2 cups of quinoa, rinsed
- 2 teaspoons of ground cumin
- 2 teaspoons of turmeric
- Salt, to taste
- 1 handful parsley, chopped

Cooking Instruction:

1. To begin, press the Sauté button to heat your Instant Pot. Once hot, add the oil and garlic to the pot, stir and cook for 1 minute.

2. Add water, quinoa, cumin, turmeric, and salt, stirring well. Lock the lid. Select the Manual mode and set the cooking time for 1 minute at High Pressure.

3. When the timer beeps, perform a natural pressure release for 10 minutes, then release any remaining pressure. Carefully remove the lid.

4. Fluff the quinoa with a fork. Season with more salt, if needed. Sprinkle the chopped parsley on top and serve.

Italian Sauted Cannellini Beans

Prep Time: 10 minutes
Cooking Time: 15 minutes
Servings: 5-6

Recipe Ingredients:

- 2 teaspoons of extra-virgin olive oil
- ½ cup of minced onion
- ¼ cup of red wine vinegar
- 1 (12-ounce / 340-g) can no-salt-added tomato paste
- 2 tablespoons of raw honey
- ½ cup of water
- ¼ teaspoon of ground cinnamon
- 2(15-ounce / 425-g) cans cannellini beans.

Cooking Instruction:

1 Heat the olive oil in a saucepan over medium heat until shimmering. Add the onion and sauté for 5 minutes or until translucent.

2 Pour in the red wine vinegar, tomato paste, honey, and water. Sprinkle with cinnamon. Stir to mix well.

3 Reduce the heat to low, then pour all the beans into the saucepan. Cook for 10 more minutes. Stir constantly. Serve immediately.

Lentil and Vegetable Curry Stew

Prep Time: 20 minutes
Cooking Time: 4 hours 7 mins
Servings: 8

Recipe Ingredients:

- 1 tablespoon of coconut oil
- 1 yellow onion, diced
- ¼ cup of yellow Thai curry paste
- 2 cups of unsweetened coconut milk
- 2 cups of dry red lentils, rinsed well and drained
- 3 cups of bite-sized cauliflower florets
- 2 golden potatoes, cut into chunks
- 2 carrots, peeled and diced
- 8 cups of low-sodium vegetable soup, divided
- 1 bunch kale, stems removed and roughly chopped
- Sea salt, to taste
- ½ cup of fresh cilantro, chopped
- Pinch crushed red pepper flakes

Cooking Instruction:

1. Heat the coconut oil in a nonstick skillet over medium-high heat until melted. Add the onion and sauté for 5 minutes or until translucent.

2. Pour in the curry paste and sauté for another 2 minutes, then fold in the coconut milk and stir to combine well. Bring to a simmer and turn off the heat.

3. Put the lentils, cauliflower, potatoes, and carrot in the slow cooker. Pour in 6 cups of vegetable soup and the curry mixture. Stir to combine well.

4. Cover and cook on high for 4 hours or until the lentils and vegetables are soft. Stir periodically.

5. During the last 30 minutes, fold the kale in the slow cooker and pour in the remaining vegetable soup. Sprinkle with salt.

6. Pour the stew in a large serving bowl and spread the cilantro and red pepper flakes on top before serving hot.

Ritzy Veggie Chili

Prep Time: 15 minutes
Cooking Time: 5 hours
Servings: 4

Recipe Ingredients:

- 1 (28-ounce / 794-g) can chopped tomatoes, with the juice
- 1 (15-ounce / 425-g) can black beans, drained and rinsed
- 1 (15-ounce / 425-g) can redly beans, drained and rinsed
- 1 medium green bell pepper, chopped
- 1 yellow onion, chopped
- 1 tablespoon of onion powder
- 1 teaspoon of paprika
- 1 teaspoon of cayenne pepper
- 1 teaspoon of garlic powder
- ½ teaspoon of sea salt
- ½ teaspoon of ground black pepper
- 1 tablespoon of olive oil
- 1 large hass avocado, pitted, peeled, and chopped, for garnish

Cooking Instruction:

1. To begin, combine all the, except for the avocado, in the slow cooker. Stir to mix well.

2. Put the slow cooker lid on and cook on high for 5 hours or until the vegetables are tender and the mixture has a thick consistency.

3. Pour the chili in a large serving bowl. Allow to cool for 30 minutes, then spread with chopped avocado and serve.

Walnut and Ricotta Spaghetti

Prep Time: 15 minutes
Cooking Time: 10 minutes
Servings: 5-6

Recipe Ingredients:

- 1 pound of (454 g) cooked whole-wheat spaghetti
- 2 tablespoons of extra-virgin olive oil
- 4 cloves garlic, minced
- ¾ cup of walnuts, toasted and finely chopped
- 2 tablespoons of ricotta cheese
- ¼ cup of flat-leaf parsley, chopped
- ½ cup of grated Parmesan cheese
- Sea salt and freshly ground pepper, to taste

Cooking Instruction:

1 Reserve a cup of spaghetti water while cooking the spaghetti. Heat the olive oil in a nonstick skillet over medium-low heat or until shimmering.

2 Add the garlic and sauté for a minute or until fragrant. Pour the spaghetti water into the skillet and cook for 8 more minutes.

3 Turn off the heat and mix in the walnuts and ricotta cheese.

Baked Rolled Oat with Pears and Pecans

Prep Time: 15 minutes
Cooking Time: 30 minutes
Servings: 5-6

Recipe Ingredients:

- 2 tablespoons of coconut oil, melted, plus more for greasing the pan
- 3 ripe pears, cored and diced
- 2 cups of unsweetened almond milk
- 1 tablespoon of pure vanilla extract
- ¼ cup of pure maple syrup
- 2 cups of gluten-free rolled oats
- ½ cup of raisins
- ¾ cup of chopped pecans
- ¼ teaspoon of ground nutmeg
- 1 teaspoon of ground cinnamon
- ½ teaspoon of ground ginger
- ¼ teaspoon of sea salt

Cooking Instruction:

1 First, preheat the oven to 350°F (180°C). Grease a baking dish with melted coconut oil, then spread the pears in a single layer on the baking dish evenly.

2 Combine the almond milk, vanilla extract, maple syrup, and coconut oil in a bowl. Stir to mix well.

3 Combine the remaining in a separate large bowl. Stir to mix well. Fold the almond milk mixture in the bowl, then pour the mixture over the pears.

4 Place the baking dish in the preheated oven and bake for 30 minutes or until lightly browned and set. Serve immediately.

Brown Rice Pilaf with Pistachios and Raisins

Prep Time: 5 minutes
Cooking Time: 15 minutes
Servings: 5-6

Recipe Ingredients:

- 1 tablespoon of extra-virgin olive oil
- 1 cup of chopped onion
- ½ cup of shredded carrot
- ½ teaspoon of ground cinnamon
- 1 teaspoon of ground cumin
- 2 cups of brown rice
- 1¾ cups of pure orange juice
- ¼ cup of water
- ½ cup of shelled pistachios
- 1 cup of golden raisins
- ½ cup of chopped fresh chives

Cooking Instruction:

1 Heat the olive oil in a saucepan over medium-high heat until shimmering. Add the onion and sauté for 5 minutes or until translucent.

2 Add the carrots, cinnamon, and cumin, then sauté for 1 minutes or until aromatic. Pour int the brown rice, orange juice, and water. Bring to a boil.

3 Reduce the heat to medium-low and simmer for 7 minutes or until the liquid is almost absorbed.

4 Transfer the rice mixture in a large serving bowl, then spread with pistachios, raisins, and chives. Serve immediately.

Pearl Barley Risotto with Parmesan Cheese

Prep Time: 5 minutes
Cooking Time: 20 minutes
Servings: 5-6

Recipe Ingredients:

- 4 cups of low-sodium or no-salt-added vegetable broth
- 1 tablespoon of extra-virgin olive oil
- 1 cup of chopped yellow onion
- 2 cups of uncooked pearl barley
- ½ cup of dry white wine
- 1 cup of freshly grated Parmesan cheese, divided
- ¼ teaspoon of kosher or sea salt
- ¼ teaspoon of freshly ground black pepper
- Fresh chopped chives and lemon wedges, for serving (optional)

Cooking Instruction:

1. Pour the broth into a medium saucepan and bring to a simmer. Heat the olive oil in a large stockpot over medium-high heat.

2. Add the onion and cook for about 4 minutes, stirring occasionally. Add the barley and cook for 2 minutes, stirring, or until the barley is toasted.

3. Pour in the wine and cook for about 1 minute, or until most of the liquid evaporates.

4. Add 1 cup of the warm broth into the pot and cook, stirring, for about 2 minutes, or until most of the liquid is absorbed.

5. Add the remaining broth, 1 cup at a time, cooking until each cup is absorbed (about 2 minutes each time) before adding the next.

6. The last addition of broth will take a bit longer to absorb, about 4 minutes. Remove the pot from the heat, and stir in ½ cup of the cheese, and the salt and pepper.

7. Serve with the remaining ½ cup of the cheese on the side, along with the chives and lemon wedges (if desired).

Cranberry and Almond Quinoa

Prep Time: 5 minutes
Cooking Time: 10 minutes
Servings: 1-2

Recipe Ingredients:

- 2 cups of water
- 1 cup of quinoa, rinsed
- ¼ cup of salted sunflower seeds
- ½ cup of slivered almonds
- 1 cup of dried cranberries

Cooking Instruction:

1 Combine water and quinoa in the Instant Pot. Secure the lid. Select the Manual mode and set the cooking time for 10 minutes at High Pressure.

2 Once cooking is complete, do a quick pressure release. Carefully open the lid. Add sunflower seeds, almonds, and dried cranberries and gently mix until well combined. Serve hot.

Israeli Couscous with Asparagus

Prep Time: 5 minutes
Cooking Time: 25 minutes
Servings: 5-6

Recipe Ingredients:

- 1½ pounds of (680 g) asparagus spears, ends trimmed and stalks chopped into 1-inch pieces
- 1 garlic clove, minced
- 1 tablespoon of extra-virgin olive oil
- ¼ teaspoon of freshly ground black pepper
- 1¾ cups of water
- 1 (8-ounce/ 227-g) box uncooked whole-wheat or regular
- Israeli couscous
- (about 1⅓ cups)
- ¼ teaspoon of kosher salt
- 1 cup of garlic-and-herb goat cheese, at room temperature

Cooking Instruction:

1. Preheat the oven to 425°F (220°C). In a large bowl, stir together the asparagus, garlic, oil, and pepper.

2. Spread the asparagus on a large, rimmed baking sheet and roast for 10 minutes, stirring a few times.

3. Remove the pan from the oven, and spoon the asparagus into a large serving bowl. Set aside.

4. While the asparagus is roasting, bring the water to a boil in a medium saucepan. Add the couscous and season with salt, stirring well.

5. Reduce the heat to medium-low. Cover and cook for 12 minutes, or until the water is absorbed.

6. Pour the hot couscous into the bowl with the asparagus. Add the goat cheese and mix thoroughly until completely melted. Serve immediately.

Gouda Beef and Spinach Fettuccine

Prep Time: 10 minutes
Cooking Time: 15 minutes
Servings: 5-6

Recipe Ingredients:

- 10 ounces of (283 g) ground beef
- 1 pound of (454 g) fettuccine pasta
- 1 cup of gouda cheese, shredded
- 1 cup of fresh spinach, torn
- 1 medium onion, chopped
- 2 cups of tomatoes, diced
- 1 tablespoon of olive oil
- 1 teaspoon of salt
- ½ teaspoon of ground black pepper

Cooking Instruction:

1. Heat the olive oil on Sauté mode in the Instant Pot. Stir-fry the beef and onion for 5 minutes. Add the pasta.

2. Pour water enough to cover and season with salt and pepper. Cook on High Pressure for 5 minutes. Do a quick release.

3. Press Sauté and stir in the tomato and spinach; cook for 5 minutes. Top with Gouda to serve.

Asparagus and Broccoli Primavera Farfalle

Prep Time: 15 minutes
Cooking Time: 12 minutes
Servings: 3-4

Recipe Ingredients:

- 1 bunch asparagus, trimmed, cut into 1-inch pieces
- 2 cups of broccoli florets
- 3 tablespoons of olive oil
- 3 teaspoons of salt
- 10 ounces of (283 g) egg noodles
- 3 garlic cloves, minced
- 2½ cups of vegetable stock
- ½ cup of heavy cream
- 1 cup of small tomatoes, halved
- ¼ cup of chopped basil
- ½ cup of grated Parmesan cheese

Cooking Instruction:

1. At first, pour 2 cups of water, add the noodles, 2 tablespoons of olive oil, garlic and salt.

2. Place a trivet over the water. Combine asparagus, broccoli, remaining olive oil and salt in a bowl.

3. Place the vegetables on the trivet. Seal the lid and cook on Steam for 12 minutes on High. Do a quick release.

4. Remove the vegetables to a plate. Stir the heavy cream and tomatoes in the pasta. Press Sauté and simmer the cream until desired consistency.

5. Gently mix in the asparagus and broccoli. Garnish with basil and Parmesan, to serve.

Chapter 5: Vegetable Recipes

Triumph of Cucumbers and Avocados (Spanish)

Prep Time: 10 minutes
Cooking Time: 15 minutes
Servings: 3-4

Recipe Ingredients:

- 12 ounces of cherry tomatoes, cut in half
- 3 small avocados, chopped
- 5 small cucumbers, chopped
- ½ teaspoon of ground black pepper
- 2 tablespoons of fresh lemon juice
- ¼ cup of fresh cilantro, chopped
- 1 teaspoon of sea salt
- 2 tbsp olive oil

Cooking Instruction:

1. Add cherry tomatoes, cucumbers, avocados, and cilantro into the large mixing bowl and mix well.

2. Mix olive oil, lemon juice, black pepper, and salt and pour over salad. Toss well and serve immediately.

Mushroom and Spinach Stuffed Peppers

Prep Time: 15 minutes
Cooking Time: 8 minutes
Servings: 6-7

Recipe Ingredients:

- 7 mini sweet peppers
- 1 cup of button mushrooms, minced
- 5 ounces (142 g) organic baby spinach
- ½ teaspoon of fresh garlic
- ½ teaspoon of coarse sea salt
- ¼ teaspoon of cracked mixed pepper
- 2 tablespoons of water
- 1 tablespoon of olive oil
- Organic Mozzarella cheese, diced

Cooking Instruction:

1. Put the sweet peppers and water in the instant pot and Sauté for 2 minutes. Remove the peppers and put the olive oil into the pot.

2. Add in the mushrooms, garlic, spices and spinach and stir. Cook on Sauté until the mixture is dry.

3. Stuff each sweet pepper with the cheese and spinach mixture. Bake the stuffed peppers in an oven for 6 minutes at 400°F (205°C). Once done, serve hot.

Black Bean and Corn Tortilla Bowls

Prep Time: 10 minutes
Cooking Time: 8 minutes
Servings: 3-4

Recipe Ingredients:

- 1½ cups of vegetable broth
- ½ cup of tomatoes, undrained diced
- 1 small onion, diced
- 2 garlic cloves, finely minced
- 1 teaspoon of chili powder
- 1 teaspoon of cumin
- ½ teaspoon of paprika
- ½ teaspoon of ground coriander
- Salt and pepper to taste
- ½ cup of carrots, diced
- 2 small potatoes, cubed
- ½ cup of bell pepper, chopped
- ½ can of black beans, drained and rinsed
- 1 cup of frozen corn kernels
- ½ tablespoon of lime juice
- 2 tablespoons of cilantro for topping, chopped
- Whole-wheat tortilla chips

Cooking Instruction:

1 Add the oil and all the vegetables into the instant pot and Sauté for 3 minutes. Add all the spices, corn, lime juice, and broth, along with the beans, to the pot.

2 Seal the lid and cook on Manual setting at High Pressure for 5 minutes. Once done, release the pressure naturally when the timer goes off. Remove the lid.

3 To serve, put the prepared mixture into a bowl. Top with tortilla chips and fresh cilantro. Serve.

Potato, Corn, and Spinach Medley

Prep Time: 10 minutes
Cooking Time: 10 minutes
Servings: 5-6

Recipe Ingredients:

- 1 tablespoon of olive oil
- 3 scallions, chopped
- ½ cup of onion, chopped
- 2 large white potatoes, peeled and diced
- 1 tablespoon of ginger, grated
- 3 cups of frozen corn kernels
- 1 cup of vegetable stock
- 1 tablespoon of fish sauce
- 2 tablespoons of light soy sauce
- 2 large cloves garlic, diced
- ⅓ teaspoon of white pepper
- 1 teaspoon of salt
- 3-4 handfuls baby spinach leaves
- Juice of ½ lemon

Cooking Instruction:

1 To begin, put the oil, ginger, garlic and onions in the instant pot and Sauté for 5 minutes.

2 Add all the remaining except the spinach leaves and lime juice Secure the lid and cook on the Manual setting for 5 minutes at High Pressure.

3 Once the unit beeps, Quick release the pressure and remove the lid. Add the spinach and cook for 3 minutes on Sauté.

4 Drizzle the lime juice over the dish and serve hot.

Mushroom and Potato Oat Burgers

Prep Time: 20 minutes
Cooking Time: 21 minutes
Servings: 4-5

Recipe Ingredients:

- ½ cup of minced onion
- 1 teaspoon of grated fresh ginger
- ½ cup of minced mushrooms
- ½ cup of red lentils, rinsed
- ¾ sweet potato, peeled and diced
- 1 cup of vegetable stock
- 2 tablespoons of hemp seeds
- 2 tablespoons of chopped cilantro
- 1 tablespoon of curry powder
- 1 cup of quick oats
- Brown rice flour, optional
- 5 tomato slices
- Lettuce leaves
- 5 whole-wheat buns
- 2 tablespoons of chopped parsley

Cooking Instruction:

1 Add the oil, ginger, mushrooms and onion into the instant pot and Sauté for 5 minutes.

2 Stir in the lentils, stock, and the sweet potatoes. Secure the lid and cook on the Manual function for 6 minutes at High Pressure.

3 Once cooking is complete, natural release the pressure and remove the lid. Meanwhile, heat the oven to 375°F (190°C) and line a baking tray with parchment paper.

4 Mash the prepared lentil mixture with a potato masher. Add the oats and the remaining spices.

5 Put in some brown rice flour if the mixture is not thick enough. Wet your hands and prepare 5 patties, using the mixture, and place them on the baking tray.

6 Bake the patties for 10 minutes in the preheated oven. Slice the buns in half and stack each with a tomato slice, a vegetable patty and lettuce leaves. Serve and enjoy.

Honey-Glazed Baby Carrots

Prep Time: 5 minutes
Cooking Time: 6 minutes
Servings: 1-2

Recipe Ingredients:

- ⅔ cup of water
- 1½ pounds of (680 g) baby carrots
- 4 tablespoons of almond butter
- ½ cup of honey
- 1 teaspoon of dried thyme
- 1½ teaspoons of dried dill
- Salt, to taste

Cooking Instruction:

1 Pour the water into the Instant Pot and add a steamer basket. Place the baby carrots in the basket.

2 Secure the lid. Select the Manual mode and set the cooking time for 4 minutes at High Pressure.

3 Once cooking is complete, do a quick pressure release. Carefully open the lid. Transfer the carrots to a plate and set aside.

4 Pour the water out of the Instant Pot and dry it. Press the Sauté button on the Instant Pot and heat the almond butter.

5 Stir in the honey, thyme, and dill. Return the carrots to the Instant Pot and stir until well coated. Sauté for another 1 minute.

6 Taste and season with salt as needed. Serve warm.

Stuffed Portobello Mushrooms with Spinach

Prep Time: 5 minutes
Cooking Time: 20 minutes
Servings: 3-4

Recipe Ingredients:

- 8 large portobello mushrooms, stems removed
- 3 teaspoons of extra-virgin olive oil, divided
- 1 medium red bell pepper, diced
- 4 cups of fresh spinach
- ¼ cup of crumbled feta cheese

Cooking Instruction:

1. Preheat the oven to 450°F (235°C). Using a spoon to scoop out the gills of the mushrooms and discard them. Brush the mushrooms with 2 teaspoons of olive oil.

2. Arrange the mushrooms (cap-side down) on a baking sheet. Roast in the preheated oven for 20 minutes.

3. Meantime, in a medium skillet, heat the remaining olive oil over medium heat until it shimmers.

4. Add the bell pepper and spinach and sauté for 8 to 10 minutes, stirring occasionally, or until the spinach is wilted.

5. Remove the mushrooms from the oven to a paper towel-lined plate. Using a spoon to stuff each mushroom with the bell pepper and spinach mixture.

6. Scatter the feta cheese all over. Serve immediately.

Chickpea Lettuce Wraps with Celery

Prep Time: 10 minutes
Servings: 3-4

Recipe Ingredients:

- 1 (15-ounce / 425-g) can low-sodium chickpeas, drained and rinsed
- 1 celery stalk, thinly sliced
- 2 tablespoons of finely chopped red onion
- 2 tablespoons of unsalted tahini
- 3 tablespoons of honey mustard
- 1 tablespoon of capers, undrained
- 12 butter lettuce leaves

Cooking Instruction:

1 In a bowl, mash the chickpeas with a potato masher or the back of a fork until mostly smooth.

2 Add the celery, red onion, tahini, honey mustard, and capers to the bowl and stir until well incorporated.

3 For each serving, place three overlapping lettuce leaves on a plate and top with ¼ of the mashed chickpea filling, then roll up.

4 Repeat with the remaining lettuce leaves and chickpea mixture.

Zoodles with Walnut Pesto

Prep Time: 10 minutes
Cooking Time: 10 minutes
Servings: 3-4

Recipe Ingredients:

- 4 medium zucchinis, spiralized
- 1/4 cup of extra-virgin olive oil, divided
- 1 tablespoon of minced garlic, divided
- 1/2 teaspoon of crushed red pepper
- 1/4 teaspoon of freshly ground black pepper, divided
- 1/4 teaspoon of kosher salt, divided
- 2 tablespoons of grated Parmesan cheese, divided
- 1 cup of packed fresh basil leaves
- 3/4 cup of walnut pieces, divided

Cooking Instruction:

1. In a large bowl, stir together the zoodles, 1 tablespoon of the olive oil, 1/2 teaspoon of the minced garlic, red pepper, 1/8 teaspoon of the black pepper and 1/8 teaspoon of the salt. Set aside.

2. Heat 1/2 tablespoon of the oil in a large skillet over medium-high heat. Add half of the zoodles to the skillet and cook for 5 minutes, stirring constantly.

3. Transfer the cooked zoodles into a bowl. Repeat with another 1/2 tablespoon of the oil and the remaining zoodles. When done, add the cooked zoodles to the bowl.

   To Make the pesto:

4. In a food processor, combine the remaining 1/2 teaspoon of the minced garlic, 1/8 teaspoon of the black pepper and 1/8 teaspoon of the salt, 1 tablespoon of the Parmesan, basil leaves and 1/4 cup of the walnuts.

5. Pulse until smooth and then slowly drizzle the remaining 2 tablespoons of the oil into the pesto. Pulse again until well combined.

6. Add the pesto to the zoodles along with the remaining 1 tablespoon of the Parmesan and the remaining 1/2 cup of the walnuts. Toss to coat well. Serve immediately.

Sautéed Cabbage (Spanish)

Prep Time: 10 minutes
Cooking Time: 12 to 14 minutes
Servings: 4 to 6

Recipe Ingredients:

- 1 small head green cabbage (about 1¼ pounds / 567 g), cored and sliced thin
- 1½ teaspoons of lemon juice
- 2 tablespoons of extra-virgin olive oil, divided
- 1 onion, halved and sliced thin
- ¾ teaspoon of salt, divided
- ¼ teaspoon black pepper
- ¼ cup of chopped fresh parsley

Cooking Instruction:

1. Place the cabbage in a large bowl with cold water. Let sit for 3 minutes. Drain well.
2. Heat 1 tablespoon of the oil in a skillet over medium-high heat until shimmering.
3. Add the onion and ¼ teaspoon of the salt and cook for 5 to 7 minutes, or until softened and lightly browned. Transfer to a bowl.
4. Heat the remaining 1 tablespoon of the oil in now-empty skillet over medium-high heat until shimmering.
5. Add the cabbage and sprinkle with the remaining ½ teaspoon of the salt and black pepper.
6. Cover and cook for about 3 minutes, without stirring, or until cabbage is wilted and lightly browned on bottom.
7. Stir and continue to cook for about 4 minutes, uncovered, or until the cabbage is crisp-tender and lightly browned in places, stirring once halfway through cooking.
8. Turn off heat, stir in the cooked onion, parsley and lemon juice. Transfer to a plate and serve.

Quick Spinach Focaccia (Italian)

Prep Time: 10 minutes
Cooking Time: 25 minutes
Servings: 11-12

Recipe Ingredients:

- 10 eggs
- 2 cups of spinach, chopped
- ¼ teaspoon of garlic powder
- ¼ teaspoon of onion powder
- ½ teaspoon of dried basil
- 1½ cups of parmesan cheese, grated Salt

Cooking Instruction:

1 To begin, preheat the oven to 400 F. Grease muffin tin and set aside. In a large bowl, whisk eggs with basil, garlic powder, onion powder, and salt.

2 Add cheese and spinach and stir well. Pour egg mixture into the prepared muffin tin and bake 15 minutes. Serve and enjoy.

Ratatouille (Italian)

Prep Time: 15 minutes
Cooking Time: 40 minutes
Servings: 5-6

Recipe Ingredients:

- 2 russet potatoes, cubed
- 1 eggplant, cubed
- ½ cup of Roma tomatoes, cubed
- 1 zucchini, cubed
- 1 red onion, chopped
- 1 red bell pepper, chopped
- 1 teaspoon of dried mint
- 1 teaspoon of dried parsley
- 1 teaspoon of dried oregano
- ½ teaspoon of salt
- 2 garlic cloves, minced
- ½ teaspoon of black pepper
- 1/3 cup of olive oil
- ¼ teaspoon of red pepper flakes
- 1 (8-ounce / 227-g) can tomato paste
- ¼ cup of vegetable broth
- ¼ cup of water

Cooking Instruction:

1 Preheat the air fryer to 320°F (160°C). In a large bowl, combine the potatoes, tomatoes, eggplant, zucchini, onion, bell pepper, garlic, mint, parsley, oregano, salt, black pepper, and red pepper flakes.

2 In a small bowl, mix together the olive oil, tomato paste, broth, and water. Pour the oil-and-tomato-paste mixture over the vegetables and toss until everything is coated.

3 Pour the coated vegetables into the air fryer basket in an even layer and roast for 20 minutes.

4 After 20 minutes, stir well and spread out again. Roast for an additional 10 minutes, then repeat the process and cook for another 10 minutes.

Chapter 6: Poultry Recipes & Meats Recipes

Pork Loin with Pineapple Glaze (Spanish)

Prep Time: 10 minutes
Cooking Time: 35 minutes
Servings: 7-8

Recipe Ingredients:
Mix to macerate:

- ½ cup of kosher salt
- ½ cup of light brown sugar, compact
- 1 tablespoon of black peppercorns
- 1 tablespoon of coriander seeds
- 4 bay leaves
- 2 teaspoons of chopped fresh thyme
- 1 pork loin (clean and fat free (approx. 3½ pounds, 1¾ kg)
- 5 garlic cloves finely chopped
- 2 tablespoons of olive oil
- ½ tablespoon of ground black pepper
- 1 pound of (½ kg) peeled pearl onion
- 2 teaspoons of chopped fresh rosemary
- ½ cup of dry white wine
- 1½ cups of pineapple juice

Cooking Instruction:

1. To macerate the pork, mix the kosher salt, brown sugar, peppercorns, coriander seeds and bay leaves with 2 cups of warm water, in a bowl, until the salt dissolves.

2. Pour 6 cups of cold water. Add the pork (it must be completely submerged in the liquid), cover and refrigerate overnight.

3. Mix the garlic, 2 tablespoons of olive oil, rosemary, and thyme and ground black pepper in the 1-Quart Mixing Bowl.

4. Remove the pork from the mixture where you mashed it and dry it with paper towels (discard the liquid). Cover it completely with the herbal mixture.

5. Preheat the pot at medium-high temperature for about 3 minutes. Place the pork, reduce the temperature to medium and seal for about 4 minutes, or until golden brown.

6 Turn it carefully and seal for another 4 minutes, or until it is golden. Reduce the temperature to low, cover with the closed valve, and cook for about 20 minutes, or until the pork is fully cooked.

7 Transfer it to a tray and set aside. Pour the wine into the same pot and let it boil at high temperature for 1 minute, or until it almost evaporates.

8 Stir constantly with the Balloon Whisk, to peel off the pork pieces attached to the base. Add the pineapple juice and onion.

9 Continue cooking at medium-high temperature for about 3 minutes. Reduce the temperature to medium, put the pork back in the pot and bathe it with the sauce.

10 Let it cook uncovered for 3 more minutes. Turn off the stove. Carefully remove the pork from the pot and slice it.

11 Top with onions and sauce, and serve immediately with your favorite rice and vegetables.

Slow Cook Lamb Shanks with Cannellini Beans Stew

Prep Time: 20 minutes
Cooking Time: 10 hours 15 minutes
Servings: 11-12

Recipe Ingredients:

- 1 (19-ounce / 539-g) can cannellini beans, rinsed and drained
- 1 large yellow onion, chopped
- 2 medium-sized carrots, diced
- 1 large stalk celery, chopped
- 2 cloves garlic, thinly sliced
- 4 (1½-pound / 680-g) lamb shanks, fat trimmed
- 2 teaspoons of tarragon
- ½ teaspoon of sea salt
- ¼ teaspoon of ground black pepper
- 1 (28-ounce / 794-g) can diced tomatoes, with the juice

Cooking Instruction:

1. To begin, combine the beans, onion, carrots, celery, and garlic in the slow cooker. Stir to mix well.

2. Then, add the lamb shanks and sprinkle with tarragon, salt, and ground black pepper.

3. Pour in the tomatoes with juice, then cover the lid and cook on high for an hour. Reduce the heat to low and cook for 9 hours or until the lamb is super tender.

4. Transfer the lamb on a plate, then pour the bean mixture in a colander over a separate bowl to reserve the liquid.

5. Let the liquid sit for 5 minutes until set, then skim the fat from the surface of the liquid.

6. Pour the bean mixture back to the liquid. Remove the bones from the lamb heat and discard the bones.

7. Put the lamb meat and bean mixture back to the slow cooker. Cover and cook to reheat for 15 minutes or until heated through. Pour them on a large serving plate and serve immediately.

Greek-Style Lamb Burgers

Prep Time: 10 minutes
Cooking Time: 10 minutes
Servings: 3-4

Recipe Ingredients:

- 1 pound of (454 g) ground lamb
- ½ teaspoon of salt
- ½ teaspoon of freshly ground black pepper
- 4 tablespoons of crumbled feta cheese
- Buns, toppings, and tzatziki, for serving (optional)

Cooking Instruction:

1. Preheat the grill to high heat. In a large bowl, using your hands, combine the lamb with the salt and pepper.

2. Divide the meat into 4 portions. Divide each portion in half to make a top and a bottom. Flatten each half into a 3-inch circle.

3. Make a dent in the center of one of the halves and place 1 tablespoon of the feta cheese in the center.

4. Place the second half of the patty on top of the feta cheese and press down to close the 2 halves together, making it resemble a round burger.

5. Grill each side for 3 minutes, for medium-well. Serve on a bun with your favorite toppings and tzatziki sauce, if desired.

Beef Kebabs with Onion and Pepper

Prep Time: 15 minutes
Cooking Time: 10 minutes
Servings: 5-6

Recipe Ingredients:

- 2 pounds of (907 g) beef fillet
- 1½ teaspoons of salt
- 1 teaspoon of freshly ground black pepper
- ½ teaspoon of ground nutmeg
- ½ teaspoon of ground allspice
- ⅓ cup of extra-virgin olive oil
- 1 large onion, cut into 8 quarters
- 1 large red bell pepper, cut into 1-inch cubes

Cooking Instruction:

1 Preheat the grill to high heat. Cut the beef into 1-inch cubes and put them in a large bowl.

2 In a small bowl, mix together the salt, black pepper, allspice, and nutmeg. Pour the olive oil over the beef and toss to coat.

3 Evenly sprinkle the seasoning over the beef and toss to coat all pieces. Skewer the beef, alternating every 1 or 2 pieces with a piece of onion or bell pepper.

4 To cook, place the skewers on the preheated grill, and flip every 2 to 3 minutes until all sides have cooked to desired doneness, 6 minutes for medium-rare, 8 minutes for well done. Serve hot.

Chicken Cacciatore

Prep Time: 15 minutes
Cooking Time: 1 hour and 30 minutes
Servings: 1-2

Recipe Ingredients:

- 1½ pounds of (680 g) bone-in chicken thighs, skin removed and patted dry
- Salt, to taste
- 2 tablespoons of olive oil
- ½ large onion, thinly sliced
- 4 ounces of (113 g) baby bella mushrooms, sliced
- 1 red sweet pepper, cut into 1-inch pieces
- 1 (15-ounce/425-g) can crushed fire-roasted tomatoes
- 1 fresh rosemary sprig
- ½ cup of dry red wine
- 1 teaspoon of Italian herb seasoning
- ½ teaspoon garlic powder
- 3 tablespoons of flour

Cooking Instruction:

1 Season the chicken thighs with a generous pinch of salt. Heat the olive oil in a Dutch oven over medium-high heat. Add the chicken and brown for 5 minutes per side.

2 Add the onion, mushrooms, and sweet pepper to the Dutch oven and sauté for another 5 minutes.

3 Add the tomatoes, rosemary, wine, Italian seasoning, garlic powder, and salt, stirring well.

4 Boil the mixture, then reduce the heat to low. Allow to simmer slowly for at least 1 hour, stirring occasionally, or until the chicken is tender and easily pulls away from the bone.

5 Measure out 1 cup of the sauce from the pot and put it into a bowl. Add the flour and whisk well to make a slurry.

6 Increase the heat to medium-high and slowly whisk the slurry into the pot. Stir until it comes to a boil and cook until the sauce is thickened.

7 Remove the chicken from the bones and shred it, and add it back to the sauce before serving, if desired.

Chicken Gyros with Tzatziki Sauce

Prep Time: 15 minutes
Cooking Time: 10 minutes
Servings: 1-2

Recipe Ingredients:

- 2 tablespoons of freshly squeezed lemon juice
- 2 tablespoons of olive oil, divided, plus more for oiling the grill
- 1 tablespoon of minced fresh oregano
- ½ teaspoon garlic powder
- Salt, to taste
- 8 ounces of (227 g) chicken tenders
- 1 small eggplant, cut into 1-inch strips lengthwise
- 1 small zucchini, cut into ½-inch strips lengthwise
- ½ red pepper, seeded and cut in half lengthwise
- ½ English cucumber, peeled and minced
- ¾ cup of plain Greek yogurt
- 1 tablespoon of minced fresh dill
- 2 (8-inch) pita breads

Cooking Instruction:

1 Combine the lemon juice, 1 tablespoon of olive oil, oregano, garlic powder, and salt in a medium bowl. Add the chicken and let marinate for 30 minutes.

2 Place the eggplant, zucchini, and red pepper in a large mixing bowl and sprinkle with salt and the remaining 1 tablespoon of olive oil. Toss well to coat. Let the vegetables rest while the chicken is marinating.

Make the tzatziki sauce:

3 Combine the cucumber, yogurt, salt, and dill in a medium bowl. Stir well to incorporate and set aside in the refrigerator.

4 Preheat the grill to medium-high heat and oil the grill grates. Drain any liquid from the vegetables and put them on the grill.

5 Remove the chicken tenders from the marinade and put them on the grill. Grill the chicken and vegetables for 3 minutes per side, or until the chicken is no longer pink inside.

6 Remove the chicken and vegetables from the grill and set aside. On the grill, heat the pitas for about 30 seconds, flipping them frequently.

7 Divide the chicken tenders and vegetables between the pitas and top each with ¼ cup of the prepared sauce. Roll the pitas up like a cone and serve.

Crispy Pesto Chicken

Prep Time: 15 minutes
Cooking Time: 50 minutes
Servings: 1-2

Recipe Ingredients:

- 12 ounces of (340 g) small red potatoes (3 or 4 potatoes), scrubbed and diced into 1-inch pieces
- 1 tablespoon of olive oil
- ½ teaspoon of garlic powder
- ¼ teaspoon of salt
- 1 (8-ounce / 227-g) boneless, skinless chicken breast
- 3 tablespoons of prepared pesto

Cooking Instruction:

1 Preheat the oven to 425°F (220°C). Line a baking sheet with parchment paper. Combine the potatoes, olive oil, garlic powder, and salt in a medium bowl. Toss well to coat.

2 Arrange the potatoes on the parchment paper and roast for 10 minutes. Flip the potatoes and roast for an additional 10 mins.

3 Meanwhile, put the chicken in the same bowl and toss with the pesto, coating the chicken evenly.

4 Check the potatoes to make sure they are golden brown on the top and bottom. Toss them again and add the chicken breast to the pan.

5 Turn the heat down to 350°F (180°C) and roast the chicken and potatoes for 30 minutes.

6 Check to make sure the chicken reaches an internal temperature of 165°F (74°C) and the potatoes are fork-tender. Let cool for 5 minutes before serving.

Herbed-Mustard-Coated Pork Tenderloin

Prep Time: 10 minutes
Cooking Time: 15 minutes
Servings: 3-4

Recipe Ingredients:

- 3 tablespoons of fresh rosemary leaves
- 1/4 cup of Dijon mustard
- 1/2 cup of fresh parsley leaves
- 6 garlic cloves
- 1/2 teaspoon of sea salt
- 1/4 teaspoon of freshly ground black pepper
- 1 tablespoon of extra-virgin olive oil
- 1 (1 1/2-pound / 680-g) pork tenderloin

Cooking Instruction:

1 Preheat the oven to 400°F (205°C). Put all the except for the pork tenderloin, in a food processor. Pulse until it has a thick consistency.

2 Then, put the pork tenderloin on a baking sheet, then rub with the mixture to coat well.

3 Put the sheet in the preheated oven and bake for 15 minutes or until the internal temperature of the pork reaches at least 165°F (74°C).

4 Flip the tenderloin halfway through the cooking time. Transfer the cooked pork tenderloin to a large plate and allow to cool for 5 minutes before serving.

Grilled Pork Chops

Prep Time: 20 minutes
Cooking Time: 10 minutes
Servings: 3-4

Recipe Ingredients:

- ¼ cup of extra-virgin olive oil
- 2 tablespoons of fresh thyme leaves
- 1 teaspoon of smoked paprika
- 1 teaspoon of salt
- 4 pork loin chops, ½-inch-thick

Cooking Instruction:

1. In a small bowl, mix together the olive oil, thyme, paprika, and salt. Put the pork chops in a plastic zip-top bag or a bowl and coat them with the spice mix.

2. Let them marinate for 15 minutes. Meanwhile, preheat the grill to high heat. Cook the pork chops for 4 minutes on each side until cooked through. Serve warm.

Macadamia Pork

Prep Time: 10 minutes
Cooking Time: 10 minutes
Servings: 3-4

Recipe Ingredients:

- 1 (1-pound / 454-g) pork tenderloin, cut into ½-inch slices and pounded thin
- 1 teaspoon of sea salt, divided
- 1 tablespoon of extra-virgin olive oil
- ¼ teaspoon of freshly ground black pepper, divided
- ½ cup of macadamia nuts
- 1 cup of unsweetened coconut milk

Cooking Instruction:

1. Preheat the oven to 400°F (205°C). On a clean work surface, rub the pork with ½ teaspoon of the salt and ⅛ teaspoon of the ground black pepper. Set aside.

2. Ground the macadamia nuts in a food processor, then combine with remaining salt and black pepper in a bowl. Stir to mix well and set aside.

3. Combine the coconut milk and olive oil in a separate bowl. Stir to mix well. Dredge the pork chops into the bowl of coconut milk mixture.

4. Then dunk into the bowl of macadamia nut mixture to coat well. Shake the excess off.

5. Put the well-coated pork chops on a baking sheet, then bake for 10 minutes or until the internal temperature of the pork reaches at least 165°F (74°C).

6. Transfer the pork chops to a serving plate and serve immediately.

Beef, Tomato, and Lentils Stew

Prep Time: 10 minutes
Cooking Time: 10 minutes
Servings: 3-4

Recipe Ingredients:

- 1 tablespoon of extra-virgin olive oil
- 1 onion, chopped
- 1 (14-ounce / 397-g) can chopped tomatoes with garlic and basil, drained
- 1 (14-ounce / 397-g) can lentils, drained
- ½ teaspoon of sea salt
- ⅛ tablespoon of freshly ground black pepper
- 1 pound of (454 g) extra-lean ground beef

Cooking Instruction:

1 Heat the olive oil in a pot over medium-high heat until shimmering. Add the beef and onion to the pot and sauté for 5 minutes or until the beef is lightly browned.

2 Add the remaining. Bring to a boil. Reduce the heat to medium and cook for 4 more minutes or until the lentils are tender.

3 Keep stirring during the cooking. Pour them in a large serving bowl and serve immediately.

Apricot Pork Meat (Spanish)

Prep Time: 5 minutes
Cooking Time: 60 minutes
Servings: 7-8

Recipe Ingredients:

- 3 pounds of boneless rolled pork
- ½ cup of ketchup
- 1 teaspoon of paprika
- ½ cup of teriyaki sauce
- 1/3 Cup of canned apricots
- ¼ cup of cider vinegar
- 1 large onion sliced
- ¼ cup of dark brown sugar, packaged
- 1 teaspoon of dried mustard
- 2 cups of water
- ¼ teaspoon of black pepper

Cooking Instruction:

1 To begin, put the creed meat in a large plastic bag or glass dish. Combine ketchup, teriyaki sauce, canned food, vinegar, brown sugar, paprika, mustard and pepper.

2 Mix together and pour over pork. Refrigerate overnight. Remove the pork from the marinade and keep the marinade.

3 Brown pork on both sides in the pressure cooker over medium heat. Remove pork from the pot.

4 Put the cooking rack, half of the sliced onion and the water inside the pot. Put the pork on the rack of the pot and distribute the remaining onion evenly over the meat. Close and secure the lid.

5 Place the pressure regulator on the vent tube and cook 60 minutes once the pressure regulator begins to rock slowly.

6 Let the pressure decrease on its own. Put in a saucepan the marinade that it kept and boil until it thickens, stirring occasionally.

7 Remove the meat and onions from the pressure cooker. Add onions to the thickened marinade and serve with sliced pork.

8 Onions can be stepped on before adding to the sauce and served with rice, if desired.

Pork Cacciatore (Italian)

Prep Time: 10 minutes
Cooking Time: 6 hours
Servings: 5-6

Recipe Ingredients:

- 1 ½ lbs. pork chops 1 teaspoon dried oregano
- 3 tablespoon of tomato paste 14 oz can tomato, diced
- 2 cups mushrooms, sliced
- 1 small onion, diced
- 1 garlic clove, minced
- 2 tablespoon of olive oil
- ¼ teaspoon of pepper
- 1 cup of beef broth
- ½ teaspoon of salt

Cooking Instruction:

1. Heat oil in a pan over medium-high heat. Add pork chops in pan and cook until brown on both the sides.

2. Transfer pork chops into the crock pot. Pour remaining over the pork chops. Cover and cook on low for 6 hours. Serve and enjoy.

Chapter 7: Fish Recipes & Seafood Recipes

Roasted Trout Stuffed with Veggies

Prep Time: 10 minutes
Cooking Time: 25 minutes
Servings: 1-2

Recipe Ingredients:

- 2 (8-ounce / 227-g) whole trout fillets, dressed (cleaned but with bones and skin intact)
- 1 tablespoon of extra-virgin olive oil
- ¼ teaspoon of salt
- ⅛ teaspoon of freshly ground black pepper
- 1 small onion, thinly sliced
- ½ red bell pepper, seeded and thinly sliced
- 1 poblano pepper, seeded and thinly sliced
- 2 or 3 shiitake mushrooms, sliced
- 1 lemon, sliced
- Nonstick cooking spray

Cooking Instruction:

1. To begin, preheat the oven to 425°F (220°C). Spray a baking sheet with nonstick cooking spray.

2. Rub both trout fillets, inside and out, with the olive oil. Season with salt and pepper.

3. Mix together the onion, bell pepper, poblano pepper, and mushrooms in a large bowl. Stuff half of this mixture into the cavity of each fillet.

4. Top the mixture with 2 or 3 lemon slices inside each fillet. Place the fish on the prepared baking sheet side by side.

5. Roast in the preheated oven for 25 minutes, or until the fish is cooked through and the vegetables are tender. Remove from the oven and serve on a plate.

Cod with Parsley Pistou

Prep Time: 15 minutes
Cooking Time: 10 minutes
Servings: 3-4

Recipe Ingredients:

- 1 cup of packed roughly chopped fresh flat-leaf Italian parsley
- Zest and juice of 1 lemon
- 1 to 2 small garlic cloves, minced
- 1 teaspoon of salt
- ½ teaspoon of freshly ground black pepper
- 1 cup of extra-virgin olive oil, divided
- 1 pound of (454 g) cod fillets, cut into 4 equal-sized pieces

Cooking Instruction:

To Make the pistou:

1. Place the parsley, lemon zest and juice, garlic, salt, and pepper in a food processor until finely chopped.

2. With the food processor running, slowly drizzle in ¾ cup of olive oil until a thick sauce form. Set aside.

3. Heat the remaining ¼ cup of olive oil in a large skillet over medium-high heat. Add the cod fillets, cover, and cook each side for 4 to 5 minutes, until browned and cooked through.

4. Remove the cod fillets from the heat to a plate and top each with generous spoonful of the prepared pistou. Serve immediately.

Fried Cod Fillets

Prep Time: 5 minutes
Cooking Time: 10 minutes
Servings: 3-4

Recipe Ingredients:

- ½ cup of all-purpose flour
- 1 teaspoon of garlic powder
- 1 teaspoon of salt
- 4 (4- to 5-ounce / 113- to 142-g) cod fillets
- 1 tablespoon of extra-virgin olive oil

Cooking Instruction:

1. Mix together the flour, garlic powder, and salt in a shallow dish. Dredge each piece of fish in the seasoned flour until they are evenly coated.

2. Heat the olive oil in a medium skillet over medium-high heat. Once hot, add the cod fillets and fry for 6 to 8 minutes.

3. Flipping the fish halfway through, or until the fish is opaque and flakes easily. Remove from the heat and serve on plates.

Mediterranean Braised Cod with Vegetables

Prep Time: 10 minutes
Cooking Time: 18 minutes
Servings: 1-2

Recipe Ingredients:

- 1 tablespoon of olive oil
- ½ medium onion, minced
- 2 garlic cloves, minced
- 1 teaspoon of oregano
- 1 (15-ounce / 425-g) can artichoke hearts in water, drained and halved
- 1 (15-ounce / 425-g) can diced tomatoes with basil
- ¼ cup pitted Greek olives, drained
- 10 ounces of (284 g) wild cod
- Salt and freshly ground black pepper, to taste

Cooking Instruction:

1. In a skillet, heat the olive oil over medium-high heat. Sauté the onion for about 5 minutes, stirring occasionally, or until tender

2. Stir in the garlic and oregano and cook for 30 seconds more until fragrant. Add the artichoke hearts, tomatoes, and olives and stir to combine. Top with the cod.

3. Cover and cook for 10 minutes, or until the fish flakes easily with a fork and juices run clean. Sprinkle with the salt and pepper. Serve warm.

Lemon-Parsley Swordfish

Prep Time: 10 minutes
Cooking Time: 17 to 20 minutes
Servings: 3-4

Recipe Ingredients:

- 1 cup of fresh Italian parsley
- ¼ cup of lemon juice
- ¼ cup of extra-virgin olive oil
- ¼ cup of fresh thyme
- 2 cloves garlic
- ½ teaspoon of salt
- 4 swordfish steaks
- Olive oil spray

Cooking Instruction:

1. Preheat the oven to 450°F (235°C). Grease a large baking dish generously with olive oil spray.

2. Place the parsley, lemon juice, olive oil, thyme, garlic, and salt in a food processor and pulse until smoothly blended.

3. Arrange the swordfish steaks in the greased baking dish and spoon the parsley mixture over the top.

4. Bake in the preheated oven for 17 to 20 minutes until flaky. Divide the fish among four plates and serve hot.

Honey-Mustard Roasted Salmon

Prep Time: 5 minutes
Cooking Time: 15 to 20 minutes
Servings: 3-4

Recipe Ingredients:

- 2 tablespoons of whole-grain mustard
- 2 garlic cloves, minced
- 1 tablespoon of honey
- ¼ teaspoon of salt
- ¼ teaspoon of freshly ground black pepper
- 1 pound of (454 g) salmon fillet
- Nonstick cooking spray

Cooking Instruction:

1. Preheat the oven to 425°F (220°C). Coat a baking sheet with nonstick cooking spray.

2. Stir together the mustard, garlic, honey, salt, and pepper in a small bowl. Arrange the salmon fillet, skin-side down, on the coated baking sheet.

3. Spread the mustard mixture evenly over the salmon fillet. Roast in the preheated oven for 15 to 20 minutes, or until it flakes apart easily and reaches an internal temperature of 145°F (63°C). Serve hot.

Baked Fish with Pistachio Crust

Prep Time: 10 minutes
Cooking Time: 15 to 20 minutes
Servings: 3-4

Recipe Ingredients:

- ½ cup of extra-virgin olive oil, divided
- 1 pound (454 g) flaky white fish (such as cod, haddock, or halibut), skin removed
- ½ cup of shelled finely chopped pistachios
- ½ cup of ground flaxseed
- Zest and juice of 1 lemon, divided
- 1 teaspoon of ground cumin
- 1 teaspoon of ground allspice
- ½ teaspoon of salt
- ¼ teaspoon of freshly ground black pepper

Cooking Instruction:

1. Preheat the oven to 400°F (205°C). Line a baking sheet with parchment paper or aluminum foil and drizzle 2 tablespoons of olive oil over the sheet, spreading to evenly coat the bottom.

1. Cut the fish into 4 equal pieces and place on the prepared baking sheet. In a small bowl, combine the pistachios, flaxseed, lemon zest, cumin, allspice, salt, and pepper.

2. Drizzle in ¼ cup of olive oil and stir well. Divide the nut mixture evenly on top of the fish pieces.

3. Drizzle the lemon juice and remaining 2 tablespoons of olive oil over the fish and bake until cooked through, 15 to 20 minutes, depending on the thickness of the fish. Cool for 5 minutes before serving.

Sole Piccata with Capers

Prep Time: 10 minutes
Cooking Time: 17 minutes
Servings: 3-4

Recipe Ingredients:

- 1 teaspoon of extra-virgin olive oil
- 4 (5-ounce / 142-g) sole fillets, patted dry
- 3 tablespoons almond butter
- 2 teaspoons of minced garlic
- 2 tablespoons all-purpose flour
- 2 cups of low-sodium chicken broth
- Juice and zest of ½ lemon
- 2 tablespoons of capers

Cooking Instruction:

1. Place a large skillet over medium-high heat and add the olive oil. Sear the sole fillets until the fish flakes easily when tested with a fork, about 4 minutes on each side.

2. Transfer the fish to a plate and set aside. Return the skillet to the stove and add the butter.

3. Sauté the garlic until translucent, about 3 minutes. Whisk in the flour to make a thick paste and cook, stirring constantly, until the mixture is golden brown, about 2 minutes.

4. Whisk in the chicken broth, lemon juice and zest. Cook for about 4 minutes until the sauce is thickened. Stir in the capers and serve the sauce over the fish.

Avocado Shrimp Ceviche

Prep Time: 15 minutes
Servings: 3-4

Recipe Ingredients:

- 1 pound (454 g) fresh shrimp, peeled, deveined, and cut in half lengthwise
- 1 small red or yellow bell pepper, cut into ½-inch chunks
- ½ small red onion, cut into thin slivers
- ½ English cucumber, peeled and cut into ½-inch chunks
- ¼ cup of chopped fresh cilantro
- ½ cup of extra-virgin olive oil
- ⅓ cup of freshly squeezed lime juice
- 2 tablespoons of freshly squeezed clementine juice
- 2 tablespoons of freshly squeezed lemon juice
- 1 teaspoon of salt
- ½ teaspoon of freshly ground black pepper
- 2 ripe avocados, peeled, pitted, and cut into ½-inch chunks

Cooking Instruction

1. Place the shrimp, bell pepper, red onion, cucumber, and cilantro in a large bowl and toss to combine.

2. In a separate bowl, stir together the olive oil, lime, clementine, and lemon juice, salt, and black pepper until smooth.

3. Pour the mixture into the bowl of shrimp and vegetable mixture and toss until they are completely coated.

4. Cover the bowl with plastic wrap and transfer to the refrigerator to marinate for at least 2 hours, or up to 8 hours.

5. When ready, stir in the avocado chunks and toss to incorporate. Serve immediately.

Cioppino (Seafood Tomato Stew)

Prep Time: 10 minutes
Cooking Time: 20 minutes
Servings: 1-2

Recipe Ingredients:

- 2 tablespoons of olive oil
- ½ small onion, diced
- ½ green pepper, diced
- 2 teaspoons of dried basil
- 2 teaspoons of dried oregano
- ½ cup dry white wine
- 1 (14.5-ounce / 411-g) can diced tomatoes with basil
- 1 (8-ounce / 227-g) can no-salt-added tomato sauce
- 1 (6.5-ounce / 184-g) can minced clams with their juice
- 8 ounces of (227 g) peeled, deveined raw shrimp
- 4 ounces of (113 g) any white fish (a thick piece works best)
- 3 tablespoons of fresh parsley
- Salt and freshly ground black pepper, to taste

Cooking Instruction:

1. In a Dutch oven, heat the olive oil over medium heat. Sauté the onion and green pepper for 5 minutes, or until tender.

2. Stir in the basil, oregano, wine, diced tomatoes, and tomato sauce and bring to a boil.

3. Once boiling, reduce the heat to low and bring to a simmer for 5 minutes. Add the clams, shrimp, and fish and cook for about 10 minutes, or until the shrimp are pink and cooked through.

4. Scatter with the parsley and add the salt and black pepper to taste. Remove from the heat and serve warm.

Slow Cooker Salmon in Foil

Prep Time: 5 minutes
Cooking Time: 2 hours
Servings: 1-2

Recipe Ingredients:

- 2 (6-ounce / 170-g) salmon fillets
- 1 tablespoon of olive oil
- 2 cloves garlic, minced
- ½ tablespoon of lime juice
- 1 teaspoon of finely chopped fresh parsley
- ¼ teaspoon of black pepper

Cooking Instruction:

1. Spread a length of foil onto a work surface and place the salmon fillets in the middle.

2. Mix together the olive oil, garlic, lime juice, parsley, and black pepper in a small bowl.

3. Brush the mixture over the fillets. Fold the foil over and crimp the sides to make a packet.

4. Place the packet into the slow cooker, cover, and cook on High for 2 hours, or until the fish flakes easily with a fork.

Grilled Lemon Pesto Salmon

Prep Time: 5 minutes
Cooking Time: 6 to 10 minutes
Servings: 1-2

Recipe Ingredients:

- 10 ounces of (283 g) salmon fillet (1 large piece or 2 smaller ones)
- Salt and freshly ground black pepper, to taste
- 2 tablespoons of prepared pesto sauce
- 1 large fresh lemon, sliced
- Cooking spray

Cooking Instruction:

1. To begin, preheat the grill to medium-high heat. Spray the grill grates with cooking spray.

2. Then, season the salmon with salt and black pepper. Spread the pesto sauce on top.

3. Make a bed of fresh lemon slices about the same size as the salmon fillet on the hot grill, and place the salmon on top of the lemon slices.

4. Put any additional lemon slices on top of the salmon. Grill the salmon for 6 to 10 minutes, or until the fish is opaque and flakes apart easily. Serve hot.

Lemon Rosemary Roasted Branzino

Prep Time: 15 minutes
Cooking Time: 30 minutes
Servings: 1-2

Recipe Ingredients:

- 4 tablespoons of extra-virgin olive oil, divided
- 2 (8-ounce / 227-g) branzino fillets, preferably at least 1 inch thick
- 1 garlic clove, minced
- 1 bunch scallions (white part only), thinly sliced
- 10 to 12 small cherry tomatoes, halved
- 1 large carrot, cut into ¼-inch rounds
- ½ cup of dry white wine
- 2 tablespoons of paprika
- 2 teaspoons of kosher salt
- ½ tablespoon of ground chili pepper
- 2 rosemary sprigs or 1 tablespoon dried rosemary
- 1 small lemon, thinly sliced
- ½ cup of sliced pitted kalamata olives

Cooking Instruction:

1. To begin, heat a large ovenproof skillet over high heat until it becomes hot, about 2 minutes.

2. Add 1 tablespoon of olive oil and heat for 10 to 15 seconds until it shimmers. Add the branzino fillets, skin-side up, and sear for 2 minutes.

3. Flip the fillets and cook for an additional 2 minutes. Set aside. Swirl 2 tablespoons of olive oil around the skillet to coat evenly.

4. Add the garlic, scallions, tomatoes, and carrot, and sauté for 5 minutes, or until softened.

5. Add the wine, stirring until all are well combined. Carefully place the fish over the sauce. Preheat the oven to 450°F (235°C).

6. Brush the fillets with the remaining 1 tablespoon of olive oil and season with paprika, salt, and chili pepper.

7. Top each fillet with a rosemary sprig and lemon slices. Scatter the olives over fish and around the skillet.

Breaded Shrimp

Prep Time: 10 minutes
Cooking Time: 4 to 6 minutes
Servings: 3-4

Recipe Ingredients:

- 2 large eggs
- 1 tablespoon of water
- 2 cups of seasoned Italian bread crumbs
- 1 teaspoon of salt
- 1 cup of flour
- 1 pound of (454 g) large shrimp (21 to 25), peeled and deveined
- Extra-virgin olive oil, as needed

Cooking Instruction:

1. In a small bowl, beat the eggs with the water, then transfer to a shallow dish. Add the bread crumbs and salt to a separate shallow dish, then mix well.

2. Place the flour into a third shallow dish. Coat the shrimp in the flour, then the beaten egg, and finally the bread crumbs.

3. Then, place on a plate and repeat with all of the shrimp. Heat a skillet over high heat.

4. Pour in enough olive oil to coat the bottom of the skillet. Cook the shrimp in the hot skillet for 2 to 3 minutes on each side. Remove and drain on a paper towel. Serve warm.

Chapter 8: Fruits and Desserts

Greek Yogurt Affogato with Pistachios

Prep Time: 5 minutes
Servings: 3-4

Recipe Ingredients:

- 24 ounces of (680 g) vanilla Greek yogurt
- 2 teaspoons of sugar
- 4 shots hot espresso
- 4 tablespoons of chopped unsalted pistachios
- 4 tablespoons of dark chocolate chips

Cooking Instruction:

1. To begin, spoon the yogurt into four bowls or tall glasses. Mix ½ teaspoon of sugar into each of the espresso shots.

2. Pour one shot of the hot espresso over each bowl of yogurt. Top each bowl with 1 tablespoon of the pistachios and 1 tablespoon of the chocolate chips and serve.

Grilled Peaches with Whipped Ricotta

Prep Time: 5 minutes
Cooking Time: 14 to 22 minutes
Servings: 3-4

Recipe Ingredients:

- 4 peaches, halved and pitted
- 2 teaspoons of extra-virgin olive oil
- ¾ cup of whole-milk Ricotta cheese
- 1 tablespoon of honey
- ¼ teaspoon of freshly grated nutmeg
- 4 sprigs mint
- Cooking spray

Cooking Instruction:

1. Spritz a grill pan with cooking spray. Heat the grill pan to medium heat. Place a large, empty bowl in the refrigerator to chill.

2. Brush the peaches all over with the oil. Place half of the peaches, cut-side down, on the grill pan and cook for 3 to 5 minutes, or until grill marks appear.

3. Using tongs, turn the peaches over. Cover the grill pan with aluminum foil and cook for 4 to 6 minutes, or until the peaches are easily pierced with a sharp knife. Set aside to cool. Repeat with the remaining peaches.

4. Remove the bowl from the refrigerator and add the Ricotta. Using an electric beater, beat the Ricotta on high for 2 minutes.

5. Add the honey and nutmeg and beat for 1 more minute. Divide the cooled peaches among 4 serving bowls. Top with the Ricotta mixture and a sprig of mint and serve.

Peanut Butter and Chocolate Balls

Prep Time: 45 minutes
Servings: 15 balls

Recipe Ingredients:

- ¾ cup of creamy peanut butter
- ¼ cup of unsweetened cocoa powder
- 2 tablespoons of softened almond butter
- ½ teaspoon of vanilla extract
- 1¾ cups of maple syrup

Cooking Instruction:

1. To begin, Line a baking sheet with parchment paper. Combine all the in a bowl. Stir to mix well.

2. Divide the mixture into 15 parts and shape each part into a 1-inch ball. Arrange the balls on the baking sheet and refrigerate for at least 30 minutes, then serve chilled.

Honey Baked Cinnamon Apples

Prep Time: 5 minutes
Cooking Time: 20 minutes
Servings: 1-2

Recipe Ingredients:

- 1 teaspoon of extra-virgin olive oil
- 4 firm apples, peeled, cored, and sliced
- ½ teaspoon of salt
- 1½ teaspoons of ground cinnamon, divided
- 2 tablespoons of unsweetened almond milk
- 2 tablespoons of honey

Cooking Instruction:

1. To begin, preheat the oven to 375°F (190°C). Coat a small casserole dish with the olive oil.

2. Toss the apple slices with the salt and ½ teaspoon of the cinnamon in a medium bowl.

3. Spread the apples in the prepared casserole dish and bake in the preheated oven for 20 minutes.

4. Meanwhile, in a small saucepan, heat the milk, honey, and remaining 1 teaspoon of cinnamon over medium heat, stirring frequently.

5. When it reaches a simmer, remove the pan from the heat and cover to keep warm.

6. Divide the apple slices between 2 plates and pour the sauce over the apples. Serve warm.

Strawberries with Balsamic Vinegar

Prep Time: 5 minutes
Servings: 1-2

Recipe Ingredients:

- 2 cups of strawberries, hulled and sliced
- 2 tablespoons of sugar
- 2 tablespoons of balsamic of vinegar

Cooking Instruction:

1. Place the sliced strawberries in a bowl, sprinkle with the sugar, and drizzle lightly with the balsamic vinegar.

2. Toss to combine well and allow to sit for about 10 minutes before serving.

Frozen Mango Raspberry Delight

Prep Time: 5 minutes
Servings: 1-2

Recipe Ingredients:

- 3 cups of frozen raspberries
- 1 mango, peeled and pitted
- 1 peach, peeled and pitted
- 1 teaspoon of honey

Cooking Instruction:

1. Place all the into a blender and purée, adding some water as needed. Put in the freezer for 10 minutes to firm up if desired. Serve chilled or at room temperature.

Grilled Stone Fruit with Honey

Prep Time: 8 minutes
Cooking Time: 6 minutes
Servings: 1-2

Recipe Ingredients:

- 3 apricots, halved and pitted
- 2 plums, halved and pitted
- 2 peaches, halved and pitted
- ½ cup of low-fat ricotta cheese
- 2 tablespoons of honey
- Cooking spray

Cooking Instruction:

1. To begin, preheat the grill to medium heat. Spray the grill grates with cooking spray.

2. Arrange the fruit, cut side down, on the grill, and cook for 2 to 3 minutes per side, or until lightly charred and softened.

3. Serve warm with a sprinkle of cheese and a drizzle of honey.

Crispy Sesame Cookies

Prep Time: 5 minutes
Cooking Time: 8 to 10 minutes
Servings: 14 to 16

Recipe Ingredients:

- 1 cup of hulled sesame seeds
- 1 cup of sugar
- 8 tablespoons of almond butter
- 2 large eggs
- 1¼ cups of flour

Cooking Instruction:

1. Preheat the oven to 350°F (180°C). Toast the sesame seeds on a baking sheet for 3 minutes. Set aside and let cool.

2. Using a mixer, whisk together the sugar and butter. Add the eggs one at a time until well blended.

3. Add the flour and toasted sesame seeds and mix until well blended. Drop spoonful of cookie dough onto a baking sheet and form them into round balls, about 1-inch in diameter, similar to a walnut.

4. Put in the oven and bake for 5 to 7 minutes, or until golden brown. Let the cookies cool for 5 minutes before serving.

Watermelon and Blueberry Salad

Prep Time: 5 minutes
Servings: 6 to 8

Recipe Ingredients:

- 1 medium watermelon
- 1 cup of fresh blueberries
- ⅓ cup of honey
- 2 tablespoons of lemon juice
- 2 tablespoons of finely chopped fresh mint leaves

Cooking Instruction:

1 Cut the watermelon into 1-inch cubes. Put them in a bowl. Evenly distribute the blueberries over the watermelon.

2 In a separate bowl, whisk together the honey, lemon juice and mint. Drizzle the mint dressing over the watermelon and blueberries. Serve cold.

Cherry Walnut Brownies

Prep Time: 10 minutes
Cooking Time: 20 minutes
Servings: 8-9

Recipe Ingredients:

- 2 large eggs
- ½ cup of 2% plain Greek yogurt
- ½ cup of sugar ⅓ cup honey
- ¼ cup of extra-virgin olive oil
- 1 teaspoon of vanilla extract
- ½ cup of whole-wheat pastry flour
- ⅓ cup of unsweetened dark chocolate cocoa powder
- ¼ teaspoon of baking powder
- ¼ teaspoon of salt
- ⅓ cup of chopped walnuts
- 9 fresh cherries, stemmed and pitted
- Cooking spray

Cooking Instruction:

1. Preheat the oven to 375°F (190°C) and set the rack in the middle of the oven. Spritz a square baking pan with cooking spray.

2. In a large bowl, whisk together the eggs, yogurt, sugar, honey, oil and vanilla. In a medium bowl, stir together the flour, cocoa powder, baking powder and salt.

3. Add the flour mixture to the egg mixture and whisk until all the dry are incorporated. Fold in the walnuts.

4. Pour the batter into the prepared pan. Push the cherries into the batter, three to a row in three rows, so one will be at the center of each brownie once you cut them into squares.

5. Bake the brownies for 20 minutes, or until just set. Remove from the oven and place on a rack to cool for 5 minutes. Cut into nine squares and serve.

Mint Banana Chocolate Sorbet

Prep Time: 4 hours 5 minutes
Servings: 1-2

Recipe Ingredients:

- 1 frozen banana
- 1 tablespoon of almond butter
- 2 tablespoons of minced fresh mint
- 2 to 3 tablespoons of dark chocolate chips (60% cocoa or higher)
- 2 to 3 tablespoons of goji (optional)

Cooking Instruction:

1. Put the banana, butter, and mint in a food processor. Pulse to purée until creamy and smooth.

2. Add the chocolate and goji, then pulse for several more times to combine well. Pour the mixture in a bowl or a ramekin, then freeze for at least 4 hours before serving chilled.

Pecan and Carrot Cake

Prep Time: 15 minutes
Cooking Time: 45 minutes
Servings: 12

Recipe Ingredients:

- ½ cup of coconut oil, at room temperature, plus more for greasing the baking dish
- 2 teaspoons of pure vanilla extract
- ¼ cup of pure maple syrup
- 6 eggs
- ½ cup of coconut flour
- 1 teaspoon of baking powder
- 1 teaspoon of baking soda
- ½ teaspoon of ground nutmeg
- 1 teaspoon of ground cinnamon
- ⅛ teaspoon of sea salt
- ½ cup of chopped pecans
- 3 cups of finely grated carrots

Cooking Instruction:

1. Preheat the oven to 350°F (180°C). Grease a 13-by-9-inch baking dish with coconut oil.
2. Combine the vanilla extract, maple syrup, and ½ cup of coconut oil in a large bowl. Stir to mix well. Break the eggs in the bowl and whisk to combine well. Set aside.
3. Combine the coconut flour, baking powder, baking soda, nutmeg, cinnamon, and salt in a separate bowl. Stir to mix well.
4. Make a well in the center of the flour mixture, then pour the egg mixture into the well. Stir to combine well.
5. Add the pecans and carrots to the bowl and toss to mix well. Pour the mixture in the single layer on the baking dish.
6. Bake in the preheated oven for 45 minutes or until puffed and the cake spring back when lightly press with your fingers.
7. Remove the cake from the oven. Allow to cool for at least 15 minutes, then serve.

Raspberry Yogurt Basted Cantaloupe

Prep Time: 15 minutes
Servings: 5-6

Recipe Ingredients:

- 2 cups of fresh raspberries, mashed
- 1 cup of plain coconut yogurt
- ½ teaspoon of vanilla extract
- 1 cantaloupe, peeled and sliced
- ½ cup of toasted coconut flakes

Cooking Instruction:

1. Combine the mashed raspberries with yogurt and vanilla extract in a small bowl. Stir to mix well.

2. Place the cantaloupe slices on a platter, then top with raspberry mixture and spread with toasted coconut. Serve immediately.

Apple Compote

Prep Time: 15 minutes
Cooking Time: 10 minutes |
Servings: 3-4

Recipe Ingredients:

- 6 apples, peeled, cored, and chopped
- ¼ cup of raw honey
- 1 teaspoon of ground cinnamon
- ¼ cup of apple juice
- Sea salt, to taste

Cooking Instruction:

1 Put all the in a stockpot. Stir to mix well, then cook over medium-high heat for 10 minutes or until the apples are glazed by honey and lightly saucy. Stir constantly.

Spiced Sweet Pecans

Prep Time: 4 minutes
Cooking Time: 17 minutes
Servings: 3-4

Recipe Ingredients:

- 1 cup of pecan halves
- 3 tablespoons of almond butter
- 1 teaspoon of ground cinnamon
- ½ teaspoon of ground nutmeg
- ¼ cup of raw honey
- ¼ teaspoon of sea salt

Cooking Instruction:

1 To begin, preheat the oven to 350°F (180°C). Line a baking sheet with parchment paper.

2 Combine all the in a bowl. Stir to mix well, then spread the mixture in the single layer on the baking sheet with a spatula.

3 Bake in the preheated oven for 16 minutes or until the pecan halves are well browned. Serve immediately.

Chapter 9: Sauces Recipes, Dips Recipes, & Dressings Recipes

Garlic Lemon-Tahini Dressing

Prep Time: 5 minutes
Servings: 8 to 10

Recipe Ingredients:

- ½ cup of tahini
- ¼ cup of extra-virgin olive oil
- 2 teaspoons of salt
- 1 garlic clove, finely minced
- ¼ cup of freshly squeezed lemon juice

Cooking Instruction:

1 In a glass mason jar with a lid, combine the tahini, olive oil, lemon juice, garlic, and salt.

2 Cover and shake well until combined and creamy. Store in the refrigerator for up to 2 weeks.

Peanut Sauce with Honey

Prep Time: 5 minutes
Servings: 3-4

Recipe Ingredients:

- ¼ cup of peanut butter
- 1 tablespoon of peeled and grated fresh ginger
- 1 tablespoon of honey
- 1 tablespoon of low-sodium soy sauce
- 1 garlic clove, minced
- Juice of 1 lime
- Pinch red pepper flakes

Cooking Instruction:

1. Whisk together all ingredients in a small bowl until well incorporated. Transfer to an airtight container and refrigerate for up to 5 days.

Cilantro-Tomato Salsa

Prep Time: 10 minutes
Servings: 5-6

Recipe Ingredients:

- 2 or 3 medium, ripe tomatoes, diced
- 1 serrano pepper, seeded and minced
- ½ red onion, minced
- ¼ cup of minced fresh cilantro
- Juice of 1 lime
- ¼ teaspoon of salt, plus more as needed

Cooking Instruction:

1 Place the tomatoes, serrano pepper, onion, cilantro, lime juice, and salt in a small bowl and mix well.

2 Taste and add additional salt, if needed. Store in an airtight container in the refrigerator for up to 3 days.

Cheesy Pea Pesto

Prep Time: 5 minutes
Servings: 3-4

Recipe Ingredients:

- ½ cup of fresh green peas
- ½ cup of grated Parmesan cheese
- ¼ cup of extra-virgin olive oil
- ¼ cup of pine nuts
- ¼ cup of fresh basil leaves
- 2 garlic cloves, minced
- ¼ teaspoon of sea salt

Cooking Instruction:

1. Add all the to a food processor or blender and pulse until the nuts are chopped finely.

2. Transfer to an airtight container and refrigerate for up to 2 days. You can also store it in ice cube trays in the freezer for up to 6 months.

Guacamole

Prep Time: 10 minutes
Servings: 5-6

Recipe Ingredients:

- 2 large avocados
- 1/4 white onion, finely diced
- 1 small, firm tomato, finely diced
- 1/4 cup of finely chopped fresh cilantro
- 2 tablespoons of freshly squeezed lime juice
- 1/4 teaspoon of salt
- Freshly ground black pepper, to taste

Cooking Instruction:

1. Slice the avocados in half and remove the pits. Using a large spoon to scoop out the flesh and add to a medium bowl.

2. Mash the avocado flesh with the back of a fork, or until a uniform consistency is achieved.

3. Add the onion, tomato, cilantro, lime juice, salt, and pepper to the bowl and stir to combine.

4. Serve immediately, or transfer to an airtight container and refrigerate until chilled.

Lemon-Dill Cashew Dip

Prep Time: 10 minutes
Servings: Makes 1 cup

Recipe Ingredients:

- 3/4 cup of cashews, soaked in water for at least
- 4 hours and drained well
- 1/4 cup of water
- Juice and zest of 1 lemon
- 2 tablespoons of chopped fresh dill
- 1/4 teaspoon of salt, plus more as needed

Cooking Instruction:

1 Put the cashews, water, lemon juice and zest in a blender and blend until smooth. Add the dill and salt to the blender and blend again.

2 Taste and adjust the seasoning, if needed. Transfer to an airtight container and refrigerate for at least 1 hour to blend the flavors. Serve chilled.

Homemade Blackened Seasoning

Prep Time: 10 minutes
Servings: Makes about ½ cup

Recipe Ingredients:

- 2 tablespoons of smoked paprika
- 2 tablespoons of garlic powder
- 2 tablespoons of onion powder
- 1 tablespoon of sweet paprika
- 1 teaspoon of dried dill
- 1 teaspoon of freshly ground black pepper
- ½ tablespoon of ground mustard
- ¼ teaspoon of celery seeds

Cooking Instruction:

1 Add all the ingredients to a small bowl and mix well. Serve immediately, or transfer to an airtight container and store in a cool, dry and dark place for up to 3 months.

Basil Pesto

Prep Time: 5 minutes
Makes 1 cup

Recipe Ingredients:

- 2 cups of packed fresh basil leaves
- 3 garlic cloves, peeled
- ½ cup of freshly grated Parmesan cheese
- ½ cup of extra-virgin olive oil
- ⅓ cup of pine nuts
- Kosher salt and freshly ground black pepper, to taste

Cooking Instruction:

1. Place all the, except for the salt and pepper, in a food processor. Pulse a few times until smoothly pureed.

2. Season with salt and pepper to taste. Store in an airtight container in the fridge for up to 2 weeks.

Orange-Garlic Dressing

Prep Time: 5 minutes
Servings: 1-2

Recipe Ingredients:

- ¼ cup of extra-virgin olive oil
- 1 orange, zested
- 2 tablespoons of freshly squeezed orange juice
- ¾ teaspoon of za'atar seasoning
- 1 teaspoon of garlic powder
- ½ teaspoon of salt
- ¼ teaspoon of Dijon mustard
- Freshly ground black pepper, to taste

Cooking Instruction:

1. Whisk together all ingredients in a bowl until well combined. Serve immediately or refrigerate until ready to serve.

Creamy Cucumber Dip

Prep Time: 10 minutes
Servings: 5-6

Recipe Ingredients:

- 1 medium cucumber, peeled and grated
- 1/4 teaspoon of salt
- 1 cup of plain Greek yogurt
- 2 garlic cloves, minced
- 1 tablespoon of extra-virgin olive oil
- 1 tablespoon of freshly squeezed lemon juice
- 1/4 teaspoon of freshly ground black pepper

Cooking Instruction:

1. Place the grated cucumber in a colander set over a bowl and season with salt. Allow the cucumber to stand for 10 minutes.

2. Using your hands, squeeze out as much liquid from the cucumber as possible. Transfer the grated cucumber to a medium bowl.

3. Add the yogurt, garlic, olive oil, lemon juice, and pepper to the bowl and stir until well blended.

4. Cover the bowl with plastic wrap and refrigerate for at least 2 hours to blend the flavors. Serve chilled.

Italian Dressing

Prep Time: 5 minutes
Servings: 11-12

Recipe Ingredients:

- ½ cup of extra-virgin olive oil
- ¼ cup of red wine vinegar
- 1 teaspoon of dried Italian seasoning
- 1 teaspoon of Dijon mustard
- ¼ teaspoon of salt
- ¼ teaspoon of freshly ground black pepper
- 1 garlic clove, minced

Cooking Instruction:

1. Place all the in a mason jar and cover. Shake vigorously for 1 minute until completely mixed. Store in the refrigerator for up to 1 week.

Ranch-Style Cauliflower Dressing

Prep Time: 10 minutes
Servings: 7-8

Recipe Ingredients:

- 2 cups of frozen cauliflower, thawed
- ½ cup of unsweetened plain almond milk
- 2 tablespoons of apple cider vinegar
- 2 tablespoons of extra-virgin olive oil
- 1 garlic clove, peeled
- 2 teaspoons of chopped fresh parsley
- 2 teaspoons of finely chopped scallions (both white and green parts)
- 1 teaspoon of finely chopped fresh dill
- ½ teaspoon of onion powder
- ½ teaspoon of Dijon mustard
- ½ teaspoon of salt
- ¼ teaspoon of freshly ground black pepper

Cooking Instruction:

1. Place all the in a blender and pulse until creamy and smooth. Serve immediately, or transfer to an airtight container to refrigerate for up to 3 days.

Asian-Inspired Vinaigrette

Prep Time: 5 minutes
Servings: 1-2

Recipe Ingredients:

- ¼ cup of extra-virgin olive oil
- 3 tablespoons of apple cider vinegar
- 1 garlic clove, minced
- 1 tablespoon of peeled and grated fresh ginger
- 1 tablespoon of chopped fresh cilantro
- 1 tablespoon of freshly squeezed lime juice
- ½ teaspoon of sriracha

Cooking Instruction:

1 Add all the in a small bowl and stir to mix well. Serve immediately, or store covered in the refrigerator and shake before using.

Lemon-Tahini Sauce

Prep Time: 10 minutes
Serves: Makes 1 cup

Recipe Ingredients:

- ½ cup of tahini
- 1 garlic clove, minced
- Juice and zest of 1 lemon
- ½ tablespoon of salt, plus more as needed
- ½ cup warm water, plus

Cooking Instruction:

1 Combine the tahini and garlic in a small bowl. Add the lemon juice and zest and salt to the bowl and stir to mix well.

2 Fold in the warm water and whisk until well combined and creamy. Feel free to add more warm water if you like a thinner consistency.

3 Taste and add more salt as needed. Store the sauce in a sealed container in the refrigerator for up to 5 days.

Peri-Peri Sauce

Prep Time: 10 minutes
Cooking Time: 5 minutes
Servings: 3-4

Recipe Ingredients:

- 1 tomato, chopped
- 1 red onion, chopped
- 1 red bell pepper, deseeded and chopped
- 1 red chile, deseeded and chopped
- 4 garlic cloves, minced
- 2 tablespoons of extra-virgin olive oil
- Juice of 1 lemon
- 1 tablespoon of dried oregano
- 1 tablespoon of smoked paprika
- 1 teaspoon of sea salt

Cooking Instruction:

1. Process all the Ingredients in a food processor or a blender until smooth. Transfer the mixture to a small saucepan over medium-high heat and bring to a boil, stirring often.

2. Reduce the heat to medium and allow to simmer for 5 minutes until heated through. You can store the sauce in an airtight container in the refrigerator for up to 5 days.

Chapter 10: Dinner Recipes

Mediterranean Rice and Sausage (Italian)

Prep Time: 15 minutes
Cooking Time: 8 hours
Servings: 5-6

Recipe Ingredients

- 1½ pound of Italian sausage, crumbled
- 2 tablespoons of steak sauce
- 1 medium onion, chopped
- 2 cups of long-grain rice, uncooked
- 1 (14 ounces) can diced tomatoes with juice
- ½ cup of water
- 1 medium green pepper, diced Olive oil or nonstick cooking spray

Cooking Instruction:

1. Spray your slow cooker with olive oil or nonstick cooking spray. Add the sausage, onion, and steak sauce to the slow cooker.

2. Cook on low for 8–10 hours. After 8 hours, add the rice, tomatoes, water, and green pepper. Stir to combine thoroughly. Cook for 20–25 minutes.

Coated Cauliflower Head (Spanish)

Prep Time: 10 minutes
Cooking Time: 40 minutes
Servings: 5-6

Recipe Ingredients:

- 2-pound of cauliflower head.
- 3 tablespoons of olive oil.
- 1 tablespoon of butter softened.
- 1 teaspoon of ground coriander.
- 1 egg, whisked.
- 1 teaspoon of salt.
- 1 teaspoon of dried cilantro.
- 1 teaspoon of dried oregano.
- 1 teaspoon of Tahini paste.

Cooking Instruction:

1 Trim cauliflower head if needed. Preheat oven to 350° F. In the mixing bowl, mix up together olive oil, softened butter, ground coriander, salt, whisked egg, dried cilantro, dried oregano, and tahini paste.

2 Then, brush the cauliflower head with this mixture generously and transfer it to the tray.

3 Bake the cauliflower head for 40 minutes. Brush it with the remaining oil mixture every 10 minutes.

Spicy Chicken Shawarma (Greek)

Prep Time: 15 minutes
Cooking Time: 6 minutes
Servings: 4

Recipe Ingredients:

- 1 pound of chicken breast
- 4 (6-inch) halved pitas
- ½ cup of plum tomato, chopped
- ½ cup of cucumber, chopped
- ¼ cup of red onion, chopped
- 2 tablespoons of lemon juice, divided
- 5 tablespoons of plain low-fat Greek-style yogurt, divided
- 2 tablespoons of parsley, finely chopped
- 1 tablespoons of tahini
- 2 tablespoons of extra-virgin olive oil
- ½ teaspoon of salt
- ½ teaspoon of crushed red pepper
- ¼ teaspoon of ground cumin
- ¼ teaspoon of ground ginger
- 1/8 teaspoon of ground coriander

Cooking Instruction:

1 Combine the parsley, salt, red pepper, ginger, cumin, coriander, 1 tbsp. yogurt, 1 tbsp. juice, and 2 cloves of garlic. Add the chicken, stir to coat.

2 Preheat the oil in a nonstick pan over medium-high heat. Add the chicken mixture to the pan and cook for 6 minutes.

3 In the meantime, combine the remaining 1 tbsp. lemon juice, the remaining ¼ cup of yogurt, the remaining 1 clove of garlic, and the tahini, mixing well.

4 Put 1½ teaspoon of the tahini mixture inside each half of the pita, divide the chicken between the pita halves.

5 Fill each half of the pita with 1 tbsp. cucumber, 1 tbsp. tomato, and 1 ½ tsp. onion.

Chicken Sausage and Peppers (Spanish)

Prep Time: 10 minutes
Cooking Time: 20 minutes
Servings: 5-6

Recipe Ingredients:

- 1 tablespoon of extra-virgin olive oil
- 6 Italian chicken sausage links
- 1 red bell pepper
- 1 onion
- ¼ teaspoon of freshly ground black
- 1 green bell pepper
- 3 garlic cloves, minced
- ½ cup of dry white wine
- ½ teaspoon of sea salt
- pepper Pinch red pepper flakes

Cooking Instruction:

1. Heat the olive oil in a skillet at medium-high heat. Add the sausages and cook for 5–7 minutes, turning occasionally, until browned, and they reach an internal temperature of 165°F.

2. Using tongs, remove the sausage from the pan and set it aside on a platter, tented with aluminum foil to keep warm.

3. Put the skillet back to heat and add the onion, red bell pepper, and green bell pepper. Cook them for 5–7 minutes.

4. Also, cook the garlic for 30 seconds, stirring constantly. Stir in the wine, sea salt, pepper, and red pepper flakes.

5. Scrape and fold in any browned bits from the bottom. Simmer for 4 minutes more. Spoon the peppers over the sausages and serve.

Chicken Merlot with Mushrooms (Spanish)

Prep Time: 10 minutes
Cooking Time: 40 minutes
Servings: 1-2

Recipe Ingredients:

- 6 boneless, skinless chicken breasts, cubed.
- 1 large red onion, chopped.
- 2 cloves garlic, minced.
- ¾ cup of chicken broth.
- 1 (6 ounces of) can tomato paste.
- ¼ cup of Merlot.
- 3 tablespoons of chia seeds.
- 2 tablespoons of. basil, chopped finely.
- Salt and pepper to taste.
- 3 cups of mushrooms, sliced.
- 1 (10 ounces) package buckwheat ramen noodles, cooked.
- 2 tablespoons of Parmesan, shaved.
- 2 teaspoons of sugar.

Cooking Instruction:

1 To begin, rinse chicken; set aside. Add mushrooms, onion, and garlic to the crockpot and mix.

2 Place chicken cubes on top of the vegetables, do not mix. Meanwhile, in a large bowl, combine broth, tomato paste, wine, chia seeds, basil, sugar, salt, and pepper.

3 Pour over the chicken. Cover and cook on low for 7–8 hours or on high for 3 ½–4 hours.

4 To serve, spoon chicken, mushroom mixture, and sauce over hot cooked buckwheat ramen noodles. Top with shaved Parmesan.

Salad Skewers (Greek)

Prep Time: 10 minutes
Cooking Time: 0 minutes
Servings: 1

Recipe Ingredients:

- 1 wooden skewers, soaked in water for 30 minutes before use.
- 8 cherry tomatoes.
- 8 large black olives.
- oz. feta, cut into 8 cubes
- 1 yellow pepper, cut into eight squares.
- 3.5-ounces of (about 10cm) cucumber, cut into four slices and halved.
- ½ red onion, chopped in half and separated into eight pieces.
- 1 teaspoon of balsamic vinegar
- Leaves oregano, chopped
- For the dressing:
- 1 tablespoon of extra-virgin olive oil.
- Juice of ½ lemon.
- A right amount of salt and freshly ground black pepper.
- Few leaves basil, finely chopped (or ½ tsp dried mixed herbs to replace basil and oregano).
- ½ clove garlic, peeled and crushed.

Cooking Instruction:

1 Thread each skewer in the order with salad olive, tomato, yellow pepper, red onion, cucumber, feta, basil, olive, yellow pepper, red ointment, cucumber, feta.

2 Put all the ingredients of the dressing in a small bowl and blend well together. Pour over the spoils.

Artichoke Petals Bites (Spanish)

Prep Time: 10 minutes
Cooking Time: 10 minutes
Servings: 7-8

Recipe Ingredients:

- 8 ounces of artichoke petals, boiled, drained, without salt.
- ½ cup of almond flour.
- 2 tablespoons of almond butter,
- 4 ounces Parmesan, grated.

Cooking Instruction:

1 In the mixing bowl, mix up together almond flour and grated Parmesan. Preheat the oven to 355° F.

2 Once the oven is preheated, dip the artichoke petals in the almond butter and then coat in the almond flour mixture.

3 Place them in the tray. Transfer the tray to the preheated oven and cook the petals for 10 minutes. Chill the cooked petal bites a little before serving.

Turkey with Cauliflower Couscous (Italian)

Prep Time: 20 minutes
Cooking Time: 50 minutes
Servings: 1-2

Recipe Ingredients:

- 3 ounces of turkey.
- 1 pepper Bird's Eye.
- Ounces of cauliflower.
- 2 ounces of red onion.
- 1 teaspoon of fresh ginger.
- 1 clove of garlic.
- 3 tablespoons of extra virgin olive oil. 2 tsps. turmeric.
- ounces dried tomatoes.
- 0.3-ounce parsley.
- Dried sage to taste.
- 1 tablespoons of capers.
- ¼ fresh lemon juice.

Cooking Instruction:

1. Blend the raw cauliflower tops and cook them in a tsp. of extra virgin olive oil, garlic, red onion, chili pepper, ginger, and a tsp. of turmeric.

1. Leave to flavor on the fire for a minute, then add the chopped sun-dried tomatoes and 5 g of parsley.

2. Season the turkey slice with a tsp. of extra virgin olive oil, the dried sage, and cook it in another tsp. of extra virgin olive oil.

3. Once ready, season with a tbsp. of capers, ¼ of lemon juice, 5 g of parsley, a tbsp. of water and add the cauliflower.

Italian Style Ground Beef (Italian)

Prep Time: 10 minutes
Cooking Time: 20 minutes
Servings: 3-4

Recipe Ingredients:

- 2 pounds of ground beef
- Salt
- 2 eggs, lightly beaten
- ¼ teaspoons of dried basil
- 3 tablespoons of olive oil
- ½ teaspoons of dried sage
- 1½ teaspoons of dried parsley
- 1 teaspoon of oregano
- 2 teaspoons of thyme 1 tsp rosemary Pepper

Cooking Instruction:

1 Pour 1 ½ cups of water into the instant pot then place the trivet in the pool. Spray loaf pan with cooking spray.

2 Next, add all ingredients into the mixing bowl and mix thoroughly until well combined.

3 Transfer meat mixture into the prepared loaf pan and place loaf pan on top of the trivet in the pot.

4 Seal pot with lid and cook on high for 35 minutes. Once done, allow to release pressure naturally for 10 minutes then release remaining using quick release. Remove lid.

Lamb with String Beans (Spanish)

Prep Time: 10 minutes
Cooking Time: 1 hour
Servings: 5-6

Recipe Ingredients:

- ¼ cup extra-virgin olive oil
- 1 t sea salt
- ½ teaspoons of black pepper
- 2 tablespoons of tomato paste
- 1 ½ cups hot water
- 1 pound of green beans
- 1 onion
- 6 lamb chops
- 2 tomatoes

Cooking Instruction:

1 In a skillet at medium-high heat, pour 2 tbsps. of olive oil. Season the lamb chops with ½ tsp. sea salt and 1/8 tsp. pepper.

2 Cook the lamb in the hot oil for 4 minutes. Transfer the meat to a platter and set it aside.

3 Put back to the heat then put the 2 tbsps. of olive oil. Heat until it shimmers. Blend the tomato paste and the hot water.

4 Mix to the hot skillet along with the green beans, onion, tomatoes, and the remaining ½ teaspoon sea salt and ¼ tsp pepper. Bring to a simmer.

5 Then, return the lamb chops to the pan. Bring to boil and reduce the heat to medium-low.

6 Simmer for 45 minutes until the beans are soft, adding additional water as needed to adjust the thickness of the sauce.

Chicken Piccata (Italian)

Prep Time: 10 minutes
Cooking Time: 10 minutes
Servings: 5-6

Recipe Ingredients:

- ½ cup of whole-wheat flour
- ½ teaspoon of sea salt
- 1/8 teaspoon of freshly ground black pepper
- 1½ pounds boneless
- 3 tablespoons of extra-virgin olive oil
- 1 cup of unsalted chicken broth
- ½ cup of dry white wine
- 1 lemon juice
- 1 lemon zest
- ¼ cup of capers, drained and rinsed
- ¼ cup of fresh parsley leaves, chopped

Cooking Instruction:

1. In a shallow dish, whisk the flour, sea salt, and pepper. Dredge the chicken in the flour and tap off any excess.

2. Heat the olive oil in a pan over medium-high heat. Add the chicken and cook for 4 minutes.

3. Remove the chicken from the pan and set aside, tented with aluminum foil to keep warm.

4. Return to the heat and mix the broth, wine, lemon juice, and lemon zest, and capers. Simmer for 3–4 minutes, stirring.

5. Remove the skillet from the heat and return the chicken to the pan. Turn to coat. Stir in the parsley and serve.

Chapter 11: Snack Recipes & Appetizer Recipes

Smoked Salmon Crudités (Spanish)

Prep Time: 10 minutes
Servings: 3-4

Recipe Ingredients:

- 6 ounces of smoked wild salmon
- 2 tablespoons of roasted garlic aioli
- 1 tablespoons of scallions, chopped
- 2 tablespoons of capers, chopped
- ½ tsp. dried dill
- 1 tablespoon of Dijon mustard
- 4 endive spears or hearts of romaine
- ½ English cucumber

Cooking Instruction:

1. Cut the smoked salmon. Add the aioli, Dijon, scallions, capers, and dill and mix well.

2. Top endive spears and cucumber rounds with a spoonful of smoked salmon mixture and enjoy chilled.

Olive Tapenade with Anchovies (Greek)

Prep Time: 70 minutes
Servings: 3-4

Recipe Ingredients:

- 1 cup of Kalamata olives, pitted
- 2 teaspoons of Capers
- 2 anchovy fillets
- 1 garlic clove 1 egg yolk, cooked
- ¼ cup of extra-virgin olive oil
- 1 teaspoon of Dijon mustard

Cooking Instruction:

1. Wash the olives in cold water and drain well. In a food processor, mix the drained olives, anchovies, capers, garlic, egg yolk, and Dijon.

2. With the food processor running, slowly stream in the olive oil. Wrap and refrigerate for at least 1 hour. Serve with seedy crackers.

Smoked Mackerel Pâté (Spanish)

Prep Time: 10 minutes
Servings: 3-4

Recipe Ingredients:

- 4 ounces of olive oil-packed wild-caught mackerel
- Zest and juice of 1 lemon
- 2 ounces goat cheese
- 2 tablespoons of chopped fresh parsley
- 1 tablespoon of extra-virgin olive oil
- 2 teaspoons of chopped capers
- 2 tablespoons of chopped fresh arugula
- 1 to 2 teaspoons of fresh horseradish (optional)
- Crackers, cucumber rounds, endive spears, or celery, for serving (optional)

Cooking Instruction:

1. In a food processor, blender, or large bowl with immersion blender, combine the mackerel, goat cheese, lemon zest and juice, parsley, arugula, olive oil, capers, and horseradish (if using).

2. Process or blend until smooth and creamy. Serve with crackers, cucumber rounds, endive spears, or celery. Seal covered in the refrigerator for up to 1 week.

White Bean Hummus (Greek)

Prep Time: 11 minutes
Cooking Time: 40 minutes
Servings: 12

Recipe Ingredients:

- 2/3 cup dried white beans
- ½ teaspoon of salt
- 2 garlic cloves, peeled and crushed
- ¼ cup of olive oil
- 1 tablespoon of lemon juice

Cooking Instruction:

1. Place the beans and garlic in the electric pressure cooker and stir well. Add enough cold water to cover the ingredients.

2. Cover, set steam release to SEALING, select the MANUAL button, and time to 30 minutes.

3. Once the timer stops, release the pressure for 20 minutes. Select CANCEL and open the lid.

4. Use a fork to check that beans are tender. Drain off the excess water and transfer the beans to a food processor.

5. Add the oil, lemon juice, and salt to the processor and pulse until the mixture is smooth with some small chunks.

6. Pour into a container and refrigerate for at least 4 hours. Serve cold or at room temperature.

Kidney Bean Dip with Cilantro, Cumin, and Lime(Spanish)

Prep Time: 13 minutes
Cooking Time: 51 minutes
Servings: 16

Recipe Ingredients:

- 1 cup of dried kidney beans
- 3 garlic cloves
- ¼ cup of cilantro
- 4 cups of water
- ¼ cup extra-virgin olive oil
- 1 tablespoon of lime juice
- 2 teaspoons of lime zest, grated
- 1 teaspoon of ground cumin
- ½ teaspoon of salt

Cooking Instruction:

1. Place the beans, water, garlic, and 2 tablespoons of cilantro in the electric pressure cooker.

2. Close the lid, select steam release to SEALING, click on the BEAN button, and cook for 30 minutes.

3. When the timer alarms, let the pressure release naturally for 20 minutes. Press the Cancel button, open the lid, and check that the beans are tender.

4. Drain off the extra water and transfer the beans to a medium bowl. Gently mash the beans with a potato masher.

5. Add the oil, lime juice, lime zest, cumin, salt, and the remaining 2 tbsps. of cilantro and stir to combine. Serve warm or at room temperature.

Greek Deviled Eggs (Greek)

Prep Time: 45 minutes
Cooking Time: 15 minutes
Servings: 4

Recipe Ingredients:

- 4 large hardboiled eggs
- 2 tablespoons of roasted garlic aioli
- ½ cup Feta cheese
- 8 pitted Kalamata olives
- 2 tablespoons of sun-dried tomatoes, chopped
- ½ teaspoon of dried dill
- 1 tablespoons of red onion, minced
- ¼ teaspoon of black pepper

Cooking Instruction:

1. Slice the hardboiled eggs in half lengthwise, remove the yolks, and place the yolks in a medium bowl.

2. Reserve the egg white halves and set them aside. Smash the yolks well with a fork.

3. Add the aioli, Feta cheese, olives, sun-dried tomatoes, onion, dill, and pepper and stir to combine until smooth and creamy.

4. Spoon the filling into each egg white half and chill for 30 minutes, or up to 24 hours, covered.

Burrata Caprese Stack (Greek)

Prep Time: 5 minutes
Cooking Time: 0 minutes
Servings: 3-4

Recipe Ingredients:

- 1 large organic tomato
- ½ teaspoon of salt
- ¼ teaspoon of black pepper
- 8 fresh basil leaves
- 1 (4 ounces) ball of Burrata cheese
- 2 tablespoons of extra-virgin olive oil 1 tbsp. red wine

Cooking Instruction:

1. Slice the tomato into 4 thick slices, removing any tough center core, and sprinkle with salt and pepper. Place the tomatoes, seasoned-side up, on a plate.

2. On a separate rimmed plate, slice the Burrata cheese into 4 thick slices and place 1 slice on top of each tomato slice.

3. Top each with 2 basil leaves and pour any reserved Burrata cream from the rimmed plate over the top.

4. Drizzle with olive oil and vinegar and serve with a fork and knife.

Potato Salad (Italian)

Prep Time: 9 minutes
Cooking Time: 13 minutes
Servings: 5-6

Recipe Ingredients:

- 2 pounds of golden potatoes
- 3 tablespoons of olive oil
- 3 tablespoons of lemon juice, fresh
- 1 tablespoon of olive brine
- ¼ teaspoon of sea salt, fine
- 1 cup of celery, sliced
- ½ cup of olives, sliced
- 2 tablespoons of oregano
- 2 tablespoons of mint leaves

Cooking Instruction:

1. Boil the potatoes in a saucepan before turning the heat down to medium-low. Cook for 15 more minutes.

2. Get a small bowl and whisk the oil, lemon juice, olive brine, and salt together. Drain the potatoes using a colander and transfer them to a serving bowl.

3. Pour in 3 tbsps. of dressing over the potatoes, mix well with the oregano, and serve with the remaining dressing.

Roasted Pearl Onion Dip (Greek)

Prep Time: 5 minutes
Cooking Time: 12 minutes plus 1 hour to chill
Servings: 3-4

Recipe Ingredients:

- 2 cups of peeled pearl onions
- 3 garlic cloves
- 3 tablespoons olive oil, divided
- ½ teaspoon of salt
- 1 tablespoon of lemon juice
- 1 cup of nonfat plain Greek yogurt
- ¼ teaspoon of black pepper
- Pita chips, vegetables, or toasted bread for serving (optional)
- 1/8 teaspoon of red pepper flakes

Cooking Instruction:

1. Preheat the air fryer to 360°F. In a large bowl, combine the pearl onions and garlic with 2 tablespoons of the olive oil until the onions are well coated.

2. Pour the garlic-and-onion mixture into the air fryer basket and roast for 12 minutes.

3. Place the garlic and onions to a food processor. Pulse the vegetables several times, until the onions are minced but still have some chunks.

4. Toss in the garlic and onions and the remaining 1 tablespoon of olive oil, along with the salt, yogurt, lemon juice, black pepper, and red pepper flakes.

5. Chill for 1 hour before serving with pita chips, vegetables, or toasted bread.

All-Spiced Olives (Italian)

Prep Time: 4 hours and 10 minutes
Cooking Time: 0 minute
Servings: 2

Recipe Ingredients:

- 2 cups of mixed green olives with pits
- ¼ cup of red wine
- vinegar
- ¼ cup of extra-virgin olive oil
- 1 teaspoon of red pepper flakes
- ½ teaspoon of ground allspice
- 4 garlic cloves, finely minced
- Zest and juice of 1 large orange
- 2 bay leaves
- ½ teaspoon of ground cumin

Cooking Instruction:

1. Incorporate the olives, vinegar, oil, garlic, orange zest and juice, red pepper flakes, bay leaves, cumin, and allspice and mix well.

2. Seal and chill for 4 hours or up to a week to allow the olives to marinate, tossing again before serving.

THE End

CPSIA information can be obtained
at www.ICGtesting.com
Printed in the USA
LVHW060151110423
744041LV00012B/408

9 781638 100713